Bringing Home the Mountain

Bringing Home the Mountain:
Finding the Teacher Within

Cathy Rosewell Jonas

Free Heart Press
Eugene, Oregon

Published by
Free Heart Press
Eugene, Oregon, USA
www.freeheartpress.com

Cathy Rosewell Jonas
Eugene, Oregon, USA
www.awakeningthespiritualheart.com

Printed in the United States of America

Cover photo, Author on the sacred mountain Arunachala in Tiruvannamalai, India.
Photo enhancement by Shree & Jaypee (Jai Prakesh SB) of Bangalore.

2013 Publishing, Reprint, Paperback ISBN 978-0-9826362-3-7
Electronic Book ISBN 978-0-9826362-2-0
Kindle Version

Originally Published in 2010:
Printing, Paperback ISBN 978-0-9826362-0-6
Printing, Hardcover ISBN 978-0-9826362-1-3

Library of Congress Number 2010926355

*To the many who have embarked on a
spiritual quest to find themselves,
may you all find the way home to your own
heart.*

Acknowledgements

M uch gratitude goes to my spiritual friends and husband who acted as readers and editors to help bring this manuscript to life. In particular, I thank Steve Jonas for his support and hours of editing. The feedback of Rich Marlatt, Bill Hamann, and Steve Jonas were invaluable and shaped the final versions, as was the professional critique and editing skills of Jessica Morrell. The guidance of Joel Morwood and the teachings of the Center for Sacred Sciences were especially pivotal on my own path to awakening. With permission, I have included many of these teachings in this book, as well as teachings by David Waldman, and others whose words and encouragement proved helpful along the way. Finally, I must acknowledge the great movement of Consciousness for bringing this book to light, in particular the powerful energy of the sacred mountain Arunachala, and the teachings of Sri Ramana Maharshi.

CONTENTS

Preface   xi

PART I: Starting on the Spiritual Path   1

One: The Beginning   3

Two: The Invitation   15

PART II: A Taste of Grace   31

Three: Dark Nights and Clear Light   33

Four: Personal Retreats   45

Five: The Heart and a Glimpse of Truth   55

PART III: The Deepening   67

Six: Journey to the Mountain   69

Seven: Going Through and Through   83

Eight: Meeting Love   93

PART IV: Witnessing the Confused Mind   105

Nine: Half Home   107

Ten: Dropping Ever Deeper   115

PART V: The Journey into the Heart Cave 119

Eleven: Fire in the Heart   121

Twelve: The Fire of Surrender   127

Thirteen: Divine Union   131

Fourteen: A Shift of Gravity   137

Fifteen: The Return   141

PART VI: Searching Beyond Experience   151

Sixteen: Mind Creeping In   153

Seventeen: The Source and the Pinhole   163

Eighteen: A Witness in India   169

Nineteen: Deathless Spirit   179

PART VII: Finding the Teacher Within   191

Twenty: Mountain Resting?   193

Twenty-One: Devotion and the End of Separation   197

Twenty-Two: Exhausting the Search   207

Twenty-Three: From Seeker to Finder   215

EPILOGUE   223

NOTES   225

BIBLIOGRAPHY   229

RESOURCES   233

Preface

In fully meeting our own hearts we discover our wholeness, and with each breath of surrender the divine union becomes complete. We awaken to the one heart, the great Heart of Consciousness.

Perhaps just once in a lifetime we are given an opportunity to fully journey into the deep recesses of the heart. For me, this happened through the process of embarking on a spiritual path, finding teachers who both supported and challenged me, and forming a mysterious connection with a guru, Sri Ramana Maharshi, even though he had died sixteen years before my birth. These events led me to a sacred mountain called Arunachala, and the ever-deepening search to discover the divine within me. While I never thought I would be a forty-something year old traveling alone to India to find herself, this is where the path to awakening led me. It is my sincere hope that by sharing my spiritual path it may help others on theirs.

This is my story.

PART I:

Starting on the Spiritual Path

One

The Beginning

*The Mountain whispered, "Quiet dear heart, you are
dancing with the Divine in your silence. Be still, the beauty
of the Mountain and the flower are the same. Stop looking
dear heart, you are what you seek."*

W alking down off the Mountain was as though something new within me was being born. The warmth of the sun soothed me, the wind acted as my guide. The tears of bliss and gratitude were evidence of my growing capacity to experience love. At no other time in my life had I felt such love. It seemed that my expanded heart was meeting the sky and I was soaring in the heavens, yet still firmly planted in the earth. It was a relationship with the divine in the form of the Mountain, Arunachala Shiva. Inward, inward, I knew this journey into the heart was only the beginning, and a current of love was carrying me back into the world. This had been my first trip to India, and I knew I would never be the same.

Many events had led me to embarking on a spiritual path (and trying to find myself in India). I was baptized and brought up Catholic. From an early age while living in Northern California, the rituals of holy mass always seemed to lull me into a deep relaxation. Lofting incense, colorful flower arrangements, and taking Holy

Communion mesmerized me. I believed that somehow God knew everything about me, yet still loved and accepted me. I took my First Communion without going to a first confession. I believed that God and I had a solid relationship without the need for formalities.

By the time my family moved to Oregon when I was twelve, we were going to church less and less. My inward relationship with God was a private matter, and I would often pray, asking for strength and happiness.

I was the third child born in our family, the second girl. My father, however, always wanted more than one son. I quickly learned that even though he loved me, I wasn't quite what he had hoped for. I was supposed to be "Michael Fitzpatrick," as was my older sister. When I was eleven, my parents started having children again, three more daughters. Although this was not in my father's plan, for me it was a godsend. My sisters and I were a source of strength for one another and would remain close throughout our lives. Besides becoming a stepparent years later, taking care of them would remain the closest thing I would ever feel to being a mother.

On the surface my family appeared to be like any other white, middle class family living on the West Coast. My mother was a well-educated, professional violinist, frequently attending rehearsals, performances, and teaching. She was the only child of alcoholic parents who were cultured, well-educated, and talented musicians. Music had always been her focus since childhood. She worked hard in all her musical endeavors, the family's main breadwinner, and was rarely home.

However, when she was home, she added a quirky sense of humor coloring conversations with puns and bad jokes, which she said she inherited from my grandmother. My mother encouraged each of her five daughters to become self-sufficient and educated, adding knowingly, "So you do not need to rely on a man."

This same household that always featured a grand piano in the living room, was often filled with tension. My father struggled with symptoms from bipolar disorder and alcoholism. He was creative with lots of ideas, although his lucrative plans and schemes often did not come to fruition. One year, our once-beautiful, old walnut orchard was the victim of his mania, after he envisioned a world-class R.V. Park in our front yard. Many of the trees were sawed down to barren stumps. When not manic or depressed, he was often angry, and/or drunk; his mood swings fast and unpredictable.

At fifteen, I started to seek emotional balance or a place of center. I sensed a place within me that sometimes felt quiet and at peace. I felt it when I listened to music, wrote poetry, drew, or cared for my younger sisters. Not knowing how to reach this calm on my own, I started to pray or wish for it.

One glimpse of inner peace came on a warm spring afternoon, perfect weather for the school carnival. It was already crowded when I arrived, making it too difficult to find my friend. Two large canvas tents in the parking lot, the two gyms, and classrooms housed various activities. While peeking into one of the tents, I overheard a girl from my class talking loudly, "You're going too fast!" A game of BINGO was in play, but she was struggling to keep up. I knew she had a mental disability from seeing her around school, although we had never officially met. Without thinking about it, I sat down next to her, gently coaching her so she could find the numbers. She would light up when her numbers were called, as though she won the game. I felt happy to be in her company, and helping her.

The two hours together passed quickly. When I left the tent, I noticed how my heart felt vast. Everything seemed so bright as if the world was filled with new colors. A feeling of aliveness filled me as the sky wearing the hues of sunset, seemed to suddenly open up. I felt completely at peace, as though all was perfect. Afterwards, I could only describe it to myself as being in a place of center. I knew there was a part of me that had a spiritual essence, however, I didn't have words for it at the time. I felt brilliantly alive.

This was a pivotal experience for me. At sixteen I became a high school peer tutor working with students with disabilities. During this time, my parents moved to Eugene, Oregon, which would remain my home for years to come. In order to graduate early so I could live on my own, I added night school classes to my schedule. Because I had several elective courses to complete, I was able to volunteer in the special education room two hours a day. The teacher seemed to take special interest in me. His praise, encouragement, and approval filled me like a dry sponge.

I also volunteered at the Y.M.C.A. teaching adults with various disabilities how to swim. While these activities helped me feel valued, our family turmoil also hit a crisis point. With a quirky sense of humor, a mere hundred dollars to get a quad, and a sense of direction, I was on my own a few months before my seventeenth birthday. Following my mother's advice about the importance of education, I graduated early from high school, landed a job, obtained student loans, and started college that summer.

Unity

On my eighteenth birthday my spiritual quest began. A girlfriend and I decided to take some psychedelic mushrooms before attending a popular rock concert by the Eurythmics. After the performance, we returned to my room and lay on the floor. I suddenly experienced an intense ringing in my ears, and then my visual screen went blank. No thoughts were arising. A small dot appeared in the far distance, then came closer. The dot turned into red ink writing my name, "Catherine" in cursive, then quickly transformed into a vivid image of a red rose.

Soon, there was a sense of my mind's eye slipping through the rose. Then, a sensation of flight followed: I flew over towering trees and mountains, visiting several mysterious places including Egypt and other places I had never been. After what seemed like a long journey, I returned to the room. I could see my body lying on the floor. It was as though I reentered my body, again going through the rose. I was filled with the sensation of absolute bliss as I experienced the full sense of my body. Tears were streaming down my face as I realized that all of the images were within me, and that I was not separate from anything or anyone.

This was my first unity experience.

After this experience life seemed to change in large and small ways. The rose became a spiritual flower. (Years later I would change my middle name to Rosewell, describing a union of the rose and a state of wholeness.) A vivid connection with life stayed with me for several months afterwards. Soon after my birthday, I moved into my own apartment. I decorated it with bright colors including posters and fabrics from around the world. When I walked on campus or downtown, I mysteriously felt connected to everyone. I wrote many spiritual poems, as well as spiritual questions, over the next few years. The spiritual search had begun.

Healing

I yearned for a deeper knowledge. To that end, I changed my major from studying health-related topics to psychology. I started taking any classes focused on personal growth and found a class called "Self-Esteem," and in my spare time read a variety of books, especially those on Zen Buddhism, and many others exploring New Age topics including lucid dreaming, rebirthing, affirmations, positive thinking, healing touch, and the power of crystals. Looking back, I realize I was searching for emotional balance and that place of center I had experienced, especially looking for freedom from suffering. This proved elusive. Although I occasionally tasted great peace, I still mostly struggled and sought out committed relationships for fulfillment. My upbringing and insecurity soon overshadowed my spiritual opening. I even tried to repeat the experience by taking psychedelic mushrooms again. While there were a few more experiences of unity and bliss, I learned that the first experience was never to be equaled, so eventually I gave up trying.

Yet, I battled a constant inner hunger to feel special and of value. Like many young women, I had convinced myself that this could only come from being in a relationship. I believed that being loved by another person was the only way that I could feel love within myself. I chose poorly and found men who were immature, battled addictions, lacked education, and were unable to share deeply on an emotional and spiritual level.

At the same time, I limited my self-exploration and declined travel opportunities to live within the confines of the relationship that my dependency had created. Even though I wanted to spend a summer in Alaska with my older sister, I didn't want to be away from my boyfriend. I always regretted not going. Despite my life going well in many ways, I often felt anxious. I eventually knew if I was going to become a good therapist someday, I needed to look within. I started counseling shortly after turning twenty. I would continue off and on for the next several years as I began the journey of self-healing.

Meeting God

By my late teens I no longer considered myself to be Catholic or even a Christian. Walking around the University of Oregon campus after class, I was stopped by a religious group. Somehow, I started arguing with them. They bellowed, "You will experience the wrath of God and go to hell if you do not accept Jesus as your savior." I felt resistance. I bantered, "If there is a God, then He or She would not send good people to hell." I then pointed out how there were different belief systems all over the world. I left them with the sting of some parting words, "Nothing exists. There is no hell, no punitive God, and likely no heaven either." They likely thought I was a lost cause, some heathen. As I walked away I thought, "That settles that. I must be an atheist." Yet I knew something existed beyond myself from my few unity experiences. I continued to write poetry, musing about the nature of reality, the Universe, and my role in it.

When I was twenty instead of traveling to Egypt, as I had been saving for, I bought my first car, a 1976 Mustang. I mostly had been riding my bike or taking the bus before this, so I didn't have much experience driving, especially one with a manual transmission. I also was ignorant on how to repair cars so the Mustang spent a lot of time in the shop, getting repairs. On a summer evening, I gave a friend a ride to her boyfriend's house along the McKenzie River, several miles from Eugene. It was dusk as I turned toward home. Along a busy highway, I waited for a long stretch of traffic to clear. Then the car stalled sideways in the middle of the road. I frantically tried to get it started, but it would not turn over. This went on for what felt like a few minutes. The scenic McKenzie Highway is known for fatal accidents, so I knew this was a situation to resolve quickly. I considered jumping out of the car, but it was now too late. Suddenly, in the distance a fully-loaded log truck was barreling directly toward me. The truck blasted its horn in quick cessation. I prayed out loud, "Oh God help me."

The car immediately started and coasted to the shoulder of the road. The truck whizzed past shaking the car and me in it, as I heard the fury of one, deep horn blast. I was utterly filled with a feeling of not being alone. I felt an incredible presence that surrounded me and was overcome with emotion. It was as though I was mysteriously baptized, washing away any doubt that there truly was a God. I don't know how long I stayed on the shoulder of the road weeping and feeling held by a divine presence. Something happened that day. I became a believer in something greater than myself. I knew there was a Presence, a God.

Quan Yin

It was not until struggling through a rocky marriage and dealing with a variety of stressful events that another spiritual opening occurred. I had been living separately from my first husband as we tried to figure out if our marriage was salvageable. It was a few days before my twenty-ninth birthday and I was browsing the aisles of a spiritual bookstore. My eyes were drawn to an antique statue of a goddess. She was delicately hand-painted with jade green and soft rose, and was holding a tiny gold vase. I was not sure what the goddess represented, but I returned three times to the store simply to gaze at it before finally purchasing her. I learned that the goddess was a Buddhist deity, Quan Yin. Quan Yin is the Chinese female manifestation of the Bodhisattva of Compassion, Avalokitesvara. Her vase holds an endless supply of the healing nectar of compassion. The statue immediately became pivotal to my meditation.

At the time my method of meditating was rudimentary: I'd burn a candle and stare at the statue as I relaxed and listened to my favorite music. Then one day as I was doing this, I felt such an ache in my heart that I worried that there was something physically wrong. After this first experience it started happening more often during meditation sessions and then, mysteriously, spontaneously throughout the day. There was a bitter-sweetness about these sensations. My heart would ache with a sense of fullness (or expansiveness). Simultaneously, I started experiencing bliss. Staring at the statue seemed to be opening my heart and I felt something stir within. It was like falling in love.

I learned a mantra that I resonated with, *Om Mani Padme Hum*, and intuitively started a visualization practice. I would visualize rainbow light coming through the Quan Yin statue then radiating my heart with healing. Then, a stream of loving compassion would radiate from me to the world. I spent many hours over the next few months doing this practice. There were many nights of little sleep following these meditation sessions, as I would somehow feel the deity's presence within my heart. Yet, oddly, the next day I felt rested. I had no guidance or teachings on this practice. Somehow there was a sense of knowing what to do.

At the time, I was seeing a therapist. I told her that I was feeling so much better and was ready to stop counseling. I described my meditations and how sometimes I went with little sleep. She was concerned that I might become emotionally unbalanced and suggested that I find a meditation group for support and guidance. I hoped to find one dedicated to Quan Yin.

A few weeks later, I walked past a store selling martial arts equipment. Surprisingly, there was a large collection of Quan Yin statues in the front window. I walked into the store, discovering there were even more statues, again all of Quan Yin. I asked the owner why there were only Quan Yin statues. She explained that she was a member of a Taoist group, and eventually invited me to attend an informational dinner. With tremulous excitement, I attended the dinner and learned from a Taoist teacher that Quan Yin was an integral part of their practice. He mentioned the many vows they kept, including strict vegetarianism, not eating garlic and onions, abstaining from drinking alcohol or engaging in premarital sex. I considered it, but decided this was beyond my level of commitment.

Tibetan Buddhism

The Taoist teacher must have seen the disappointment in my eyes, as by then my heart was devoted to Quan Yin. He suggested I check out Tibetan Buddhism explaining that they also had a devotional practice dedicated to Chenrezig, a Tibetan male manifestation of

Avalokitesvara and embodiment of compassion. He explained that the mantra is slightly different with the Chenrezig practice, *Om Mani Padme Hung*, but clearly similar. Soon, I found my first Tibetan Buddhist group and practiced with the *sangha* for about a year. I learned that *sangha* is a Sanskrit word for a spiritual community or gathering.

Amazed, I discovered there were similarities between the visualization practices I had been doing on my own and the formal deity practices in Tibetan Buddhism. I wondered how it was that I stumbled into these practices without any formal teaching. I soon gave up trying to explain it to myself. My available funds often went to buy wall hangings of deities, statues, and attending empowerments since I was told empowerments were an important aspect of developing a spiritual practice. An empowerment is an elaborate Buddhist ceremony, where a qualified teacher endows permission to students to visualize themselves as a deity, such as the Buddha, Chenrezig, or a goddess of compassion. Without this empowerment, a student may risk accumulating negative karma. Only then could I visualize myself as the Buddha or another deity, and deepen my compassion. I met many Tibetan teachers during this time and was given the Buddhist name, Tenpa Drolma.

A year later I left to join another Tibetan Buddhist group that focused their practice around Red Tara, yet another deity of compassion. I enjoyed how they would chant and sing beautiful mantras to her. I stayed with this group for a year. Also, I had developed a connection to the Dalai Lama during this time, flew to California to attend a conference at which he spoke, and came close to flying to Dharamsala, India to try to gain an audience with him.

I was working in a mental health agency at the time, and explored ways to integrate my spiritual practice while at work. It was easiest when I was sitting in staff meetings, more difficult when leading activities and handling the typical stress of my job. I would silently repeat my mantra, or focus on the sensations of my heart space. I tried to remember to bring greater tenderness and self-insight to my job, and would work on this for years.

Life Goes On

I got divorced in 1995 (after a challenging six-year relationship) and formally left the Tibetan Buddhist sangha a year later. I met another Tibetan Buddhist teacher, Geshe Ngagwang Jangchup, shortly after, and would study with him informally for another year. Geshe would travel to southern Oregon when visiting from India, and I would drive down to see him. We would keep in touch through letters when he was in India. He was generous and kind, and the most accessible teacher I had ever met. Once, he tried to help me find a spiritual book he had recommended. Geshe's shaven head, simple sandals, dark red robe, and beaming face attracted many curious stares, and smiles. We combed Ashland's bookstores and cafés as though we were best friends. I kept in touch with him for years and even made plans to visit the Lingshed Nunnery Project he founded in Ladakh, located within the secluded mountainous region of India's most northern border. However, I never made the trip because I was too afraid to travel alone to this remote area when my travel companion changed her plans.

Instead of going to India, I used the money I had been saving to buy my first house, and returned to simply living a householder's life once more, meaning working and attending to the demands of everyday affairs became my priority. Despite feeling a devotional connection to the Dalai Lama and loving the rituals associated with Tibetan Buddhism, I would not return to Tibetan Buddhism until years later. I had become disillusioned with structured spiritual practices and never progressed to become a disciplined meditator. In fact, I never learned how to meditate in those years. Neither of the groups I attended taught beginning meditation techniques, such as following your breath, so I always felt awkward when we were just sitting still. Geshe helped me understand more of the Tibetan Buddhist teachings, but when it came to meditating, I was lost.

I didn't know what to do. I felt too embarrassed to ask for guidance. My mind was either busy with thoughts, or sleepy when I would try to relax. It was easier to visualize deities and chant mantras (or sacred sutras) than it was to try and sit still with a blank mind. Self-conscious, I would imagine that everyone else but me was sitting with a calm and peaceful mind.

For the next five years after leaving Tibetan Buddhism, I continued a mantra practice dedicated to Quan Yin and Chenrezig as well as read a variety of spiritual books now and again. However, in reality I did not have much of a spiritual practice. In 1998, at thirty-two, I married my second husband (my wonderful Steve) and became a stepmother to his daughter Madeline who was eight at the time. I had also just entered graduate school, studying Social Work.

Despite my mantra practice and trying to feel compassion toward others, I struggled with many relationships, including being a stepparent. I tried to balance my spiritual desire of being of benefit to others, with trying to be best at whatever I was occupied with. Being a perfectionist and sometimes insecure, being compassionate towards myself were naturally at odds. I was often impatient and judgmental of myself, and as a result, of others. It was not until I matured emotionally and finished my Masters that I felt motivated to return to a spiritual practice.

Offering Water

Besides my mantra practice, I also maintained an altar. This might seem odd since I still had little or no desire to sit formally and meditate. Yet, I somehow still felt the presence of the Divine within me. My daily practice, besides saying mantras, was to simply offer water. I bought a small silver sugar bowl from an antique store for this purpose. I would pour fresh water into the bowl and say a quick prayer as an offering. This was a practice that I continued for several years. Eventually, I stopped my regular mantra practices, and after my awakening, I eventually stopped the water offering.

In Tibetan Buddhism, altars are typically elaborate. They often include several bowls filled with different elements including water, flowers, grains, and even milk. With these offerings a prayer is said to invite all deities and beings from all realms (such as gods, hungry ghosts and animals) to accept the offering, and that all beings are freed from suffering, and obtain happiness and nirvana. My offering was simple in comparison, just a wish for all beings to be happy and free from suffering, adding that I too would like to be of benefit to others.

Separate Paths

When Steve and I met he had a formal meditation practice. I felt shy and awkward to be seen making my altar offerings, but continued with the practice, often quickly as to not be noticed. Sharing myself spiritually called for a deeper level of intimacy than what we had in our relationship. Steve could see that I was often stressed because of my job, while learning how to be a stepparent, and juggling my school schedule. I was still working at my mental health job, and also completing internships. I was busy. He would often encourage me to "get a spiritual practice and meditate." This didn't help. I did not know how to simply sit still and meditate, but I knew this was hard to explain after practicing Tibetan Buddhism.

We did not have a mutual spiritual language, which limited us in sharing our paths with each other. So in the end, Steve was the meditator and I kept my practice private. And the more Steve would nag me about needing to meditate, the more I resisted. I didn't want to be accountable to him if I was not actively meditating. So this standoff continued. It would be four years into our relationship before we started to develop a spiritual language and could share our paths with each other.

Two

The Invitation

*A spiritual practice can simply begin by learning to be
present with who we are, without trying to change anything.
We just notice the unchanging presence within and rest
attention there.*

W hen I was thirty-five my schedule was less hectic and I was
happily married. After graduating with a Masters in Social
Work in 2001, I gave notice at my job. I had been working with the
mentally ill for a prestigious agency (a position I had coveted for
many years), but I knew this was no longer the right environment. If
I was to grow deeper on an emotional and spiritual level, I
intuitively sensed that I needed to move on. I left without another
job lined up, something I had never done before. The Universe
provided and I was hired full-time as a hospital medical social
worker two weeks later.

My husband and I were attending services at the Unity Church
regularly, and slowly this rekindled a desire for greater self-
exploration. A specific Unity service was especially pivotal for me,
and brought forth something within me. I wrote a journal entry
about it: "A journey has begun within my soul. To call it the
beginning of what I sense will be an awakening is probably
accurate. It started with a talk about Advent by Nola Woodbury, the

assistant minister. I had heard that word before but never like this year did it have so much meaning for me. Bringing the Christ-Nature alive within me became a deeply felt but rarely spoken mantra. Since going to Unity, I have started to feel a sense of interconnectedness grow within me."

Mysteriously during services, especially during singing or sacred silence, I started to experience an overflowing sense of love and compassion flooding through me. Songs that pointed to the greater meaning of God, peace, love, and the importance of being compassionate were the biggest triggers, as well as attending Taize Services (devotional singing and healing touch). Often these sensations would overtake me and I could barely continue to sing, or I would need to stop myself. I could feel how the tears were on the verge of welling up, and soon were flowing down my cheeks. At first I felt self-conscious that someone might witness my tears. The singing seemed to be opening my heart, and was reminiscent of my connection to the Quan Yin statue years earlier. After a few weeks, I started to welcome the floodings. I also started to consciously bring these sensations into my heart center and let the love I felt inside radiate for the benefit, healing, and grace of peace for all. My prayer was that I be a vehicle for peace and love, and that I be cleansed of all hatred and resentment for the benefit of all.

By the autumn of 2002 the five-year dormancy that had overtaken me spiritually apparently was coming to an end. Steve gave me the *Power of Now*, a book by Eckhart Tolle[1] in October. Soon after, he learned about a Power of Now study group that the Unity Church was offering and encouraged me to attend. The group was already in progress, but I attended the last three sessions offered. I became friends with the facilitator, David Skinner (Dai), whom I would connect with in India two years later. I also volunteered to host a Power of Now study group that met for another ten weeks in our home. Before long, there was an almost immediate return to my spiritual seeking. In addition to attending Unity Services, I even returned to the path of Tibetan and Zen Buddhism, this time learning how to meditate by focusing on the breath as an object of concentration. I was soon reading spiritual

books again and meditating almost daily. It was as though my
spirituality had been just under the surface but had never
disappeared.

Ramana Maharshi

In late December my husband and I also started attending The
Center for Sacred Sciences[2], which we have continued to do. The
spiritual director is Joel Morwood.[3] The Center at that time was
located in Joel's home. Joel is rather unassuming, and often wears a
brown and white poncho while teaching. His lingering smoker's
cough from a previous habit, hearty laugh, and New York accent
either quickly puts you at ease, or makes you question your
interpretation of an enlightened person, or possibly both. Leaving a
successful career in Hollywood as a movie executive in order to
follow his spiritual path, he now teaches as a labor of love. Joel is
just an ordinary man with an incredible vocabulary, a great mind for
weaving together the teachings of the great mystics, and a heart of
selfless service in his willingness to help spiritual seekers find their
way home.

At the Center we were soon introduced to the path of Advaita
Vedanta[4] or the non-dual teachings. This introduction came in the
form of watching a video our second week of attendance. The
subject of the video was the teachings of Bhagavan Sri Ramana
Maharshi[5] (who I will lovingly call Ramana Maharshi or Ramana in
subsequent chapters). I had never had a guru before, but when I
watched this video I mysteriously knew Ramana Maharshi was
mine.

Although Ramana died in 1950 there was vitality that radiated
from the photos of him. It was as though I had seen his loving and
all-accepting eyes before, and looking in them gave me a sense of
absolute peace and comfort. The video, and in particular his

teachings on self-inquiry (e.g., asking oneself the question, "Who am I?"), seemed oddly familiar. Again, this was not something the mind could understand. While watching the video that morning I experienced a great sense of awe that I was even seeing this man on the screen. Tears of devotion flowed down my cheeks and my heart was pounding. I did not understand what was happening but a connection was certainly made. Ramana Maharshi was my guru and I knew it.

Ever since I was a girl my dreams have been vivid. As a child I would often dream of flying or swimming through water reeds as though I were a dolphin. When I was practicing Tibetan Buddhism there were several dreams of being visited by the Dalai Lama. After watching the video on Ramana Maharshi I had two vivid dreams of Ramana within a few weeks of each other. The first was of Ramana as a baby with an old man's face. He was in a crib smiling and looking up at me, and I was caring for him as my own child. The second was of Ramana greeting me with arms open. He hugged me and affectionately said, "Welcome Home." There would be a few more dreams of Ramana, however the connection would continue to grow in the silence of my Heart. This devotion would eventually lead me to visit his ashram in India.

Soon after this meeting, I changed my mantra to *Om Namo Bhagavate Sri Ramanaya*, one dedicated to Ramana. The mantra seemed to echo and resound within me often during the day, like a companion. It would relax me. I would repeat it when I spotted a dead animal, when I would witness someone suffering, or when feeling stressed working in the busy hospital setting. When not using the mantra, I paid attention to my breath. I discovered that breathing in slowly and relaxing into the simple sensations of breathing was just as successful as the mantra practice. Both of these methods led to the place of center I once wished for.

Finding a Spiritual Home

Besides our introduction to the teachings of Ramana Maharshi, Steve and I agreed we had found a spiritual home at the Center. This spiritual home would give us what we needed to develop in our relationship, a common spiritual language. However, I was not sure if the Center was the exclusive place I should attend. I decided that I would proceed full force into an eclectic spiritual path and see what came about. Soon, I was attending two meditation groups and Taize services at the Unity Church. I was also attending a new Tibetan Buddhist group, Zen Buddhism meditation sessions, and a variety of community-sponsored spiritual gatherings. Steve and I were also attending Sunday meetings at the Center. At first, I attended back-to-back services each Sunday morning, beginning with the Unity service followed by the Center. I was writing in my journal and logging my dreams. Within a few months life had taken a dramatic turn from a passive, inactive spiritual life to one that was active nearly every day of the week.

After about three months into my self-inquiry practice, I reached a decisive point. It was time to choose a spiritual home, and time to place my faith in a primary spiritual teacher. I went to the Center and asked Joel about my growing confusion since beginning the self-inquiry practice. Ramana's teachings describe that there is a difference between the Self, the 'I,' which is capitalized, and the self, which is written lower-case. The Self is also known as God, Brahman, the Heart, Truth, the Divine, Christ-Nature, the Mystery, Love, Presence, Shiva, Grace, Awareness, and the many other terms that describe the one unified Consciousness. It is to discover this Self within and recognize this as our true nature, which leads to self-realization.

The self looks toward thoughts, particularly to past and future thinking, to help define who we are. Ego attachments and a feeling of separateness from God limit the self, keeping it from realizing itself as the Self. I was becoming confused as to what I was supposed to be looking for. For me, asking the question, "Who am I?" during meditation had led to several more questions such as: Was there a God? Are there truly deities? Who am I praying to? Is all this part of Brahman (the Absolute)? Is the gap or energy between thoughts where the great gurus reside? I asked Joel these questions.

Joel answered, "If it is useful and helpful to pray to deities or God, then do it and believe in it. If it is not helpful, then don't." He went on to say that there was no way the mind can understand the phenomena of the Universe and said, "Don't even try." He suggested that I was trying to put it all into a box of perfect understanding and reminded me that Consciousness/God cannot be fit into a box. Then another person in the group asked, "What is reality?" Joel answered that each person needs to discover this for him or herself. He said, "It is not different for everyone (the true reality), nor will the experience of it be exactly the same."

I went home believing that there were so many paradoxes, so many mysteries. I didn't get it. However, I was inspired to learn more from Joel. He explained that *mystic* meant mystery, so I would not be able to find answers by solely relying on my thoughts. This somehow made sense to me. Joel also explained that Buddhism brings a person to spaciousness/emptiness, but self-inquiry helps a seeker find out whom one truly is. Meanwhile, my Tibetan Buddhism teacher warned me to not spread myself too thin on the spiritual path. I wondered whether it was time to simplify my path. Was I slowing my spiritual progress by attending both the Tibetan Buddhist group and the Center at the same time?

About a month later I was at a crossroads. I was meditating twice daily, especially focusing on self-inquiry. My devotion for Ramana only seemed to be deepening. I was going to the Center regularly and attending the Tibetan Buddhist group at least once weekly. One day I suddenly knew it was time to stop being part of the Tibetan Buddhist group. Partly this was because they wanted me to start going through empowerments.

I believed I was being led in such a different direction. To have empowerments so I could visualize myself as the Medicine Buddha, Green Tara, or other deities seemed like a step backwards. I received so many in the past, and though they were beautiful, I cannot say I understood them or was able to continue any of the practices. More accurately, I probably was not ready for them spiritually or emotionally. Now, I felt strongly that if I were to gain depth in my spiritual practice I needed to focus solely on the self-inquiry meditation, go to the Center, and start attending silent retreats.

Leaving the Tibetan Buddhist group was emotionally difficult. I was attached to the teacher who seemed genuinely interested in my spiritual progress. The *sangha* had been welcoming and I absolutely adored the beautiful shrine room. I closed my hands in prayer and slowly bowed with great devotion, gazing once more at the large loving photograph of His Holiness the Dalai Lama. This was my farewell.

My teacher questioned my motives for discontinuing my practice, suggesting that it must have something to do with my husband. "You're karma is so strong for Tibetan Buddhism I know you will be back in four months time," he told me confidently.

I explained how I was leaving so I could focus solely on self-inquiry and explained my devotion toward Ramana Maharshi. I assured him that I was going to continue my spiritual practice, but just in a different way. He did not seem to buy it. Again, he told me I would return. It made me question myself briefly as I believed him to be a spiritual authority. However, I quickly returned to my own knowing. It was as though I was being led in an unknown direction.

All I could do was trust the wisdom of my own heart even though there was no promise of a positive outcome.

Nothing Found

Despite over three months of practicing self-inquiry, any revelations of my true nature remained hidden. However, my meditations suddenly improved in March. I added focusing and following the breath into the heart center to the technique. Before this, I was still becoming seduced by the mind's answers to the question "Who am I?" rather than allowing the answer to reveal itself through direct knowledge or experiential understanding. One meditation experience in particular is worth noting. After repeating a few series of mantras and prayers that all beings would be free from suffering, I focused intensely on my heart center and breathing so much it almost hurt. I repeated the question, "Who am I?" straining for an answer.

No words came.

I suddenly experienced nothingness so intensely that it nearly brought me to tears. I realized that my life as I have known it had been nothing but an illusion. I was nothing. I ended the meditation trying to remember that we are all part of the Absolute Consciousness, but these were only words. The ultimate realization was that I was nothing. I wondered if I would experience that I was also everything, as being nothing didn't give me much to hold onto. I felt empty.

Learning to Meditate

Learning how to meditate was an important aspect to the spiritual deepening that was beginning within me. I must credit my Tibetan Buddhism teacher regarding this, since he taught his students basic meditation techniques. Joel at the Center for Sacred Sciences was also influential. Joel encourages his students to learn to meditate with their eyes open. At first this was difficult for me, since I had learned to visualize deities, which is easiest to do with your eyes closed. Before meditating with the eyes open, I battled with sleepiness since meditating can be relaxing and calming. Joel, when referring to a relaxation style of meditation, often smiles as he warns his students, "While this type of meditation is good for lowering blood pressure and decreasing stress, it is unlikely that it will lead to gaining spiritual insights."

Joel also teaches that following the breath with our attention is a technique without theological baggage. A person does not need to be Buddhist, or in fact practice any religion, since our breath is with us always. Once a person establishes a regular meditation practice, it can then take place any time and anywhere, whether the meditator is engaged in active meditating or going about his or her day. We simply relax, are present to what is happening now rather than resisting what is occurring, and just breathe.

At first, I struggled with sleepiness or laxity until I realized I was trying too hard to meditate, putting in too much effort. Gradually, I discovered that meditation was something that occurred naturally if a person simply slows down to be present to what is. Everything is an opportunity to experience this. In present awareness, I came to understand that meditation was effortless and the clarity gradually deepened. When I first started meditating years ago, I wasn't motivated to create a regular practice. I would meditate occasionally or for a few days in a row and stop for months at a time. Now at thirty-six, I found it easy to maintain a meditation practice. I attribute this to learning not to make meditation difficult.

Of course, there are some important meditation techniques I learned such as following the breath, which is rooted in techniques of Vipassana also known as insight meditation. The technique requires that a person is mindful of the breath coming in and out without trying to control it. It is a practice of being with what is despite the emotions, bodily sensations, or judgments (thoughts) that arise. The person is instructed to simply watch, observe, and experience what is arising rather than becoming identified or lost in thoughts. Each time there is distraction (usually a thought), you simply return attention to the breath. In this acceptance of what is, there is a greater opportunity to experience the crispness of phenomena arising and passing away, thus building insight into the nature of impermanence.

After learning to stabilize attention by following my breath, my main meditation practice gradually progressed to just resting in spaciousness or spacious awareness. The precursor of this was developing a solid choiceless awareness meditation, which is simply being attentive to whatever is arising. Whether it is sounds, sights, sensations or other sensory phenomenon the only goal is not to get lost in thought, or an interpretation or labeling of what is arising. Thoughts were only a distraction or a problem if I got lost in a story about them. Otherwise, thoughts were nothing more than passing clouds in the clear blue sky of Consciousness. Instructions for breath awareness and bringing mindfulness into daily life, and the choiceless awareness meditation are as follows:

Breath Awareness Meditation & Bringing Mindfulness into Daily Life

1. Find a posture that will support alertness, such as sitting upright with legs crossed or in a chair.
2. Set an intention to meditate for a certain amount of time, and stick to it. A meditation can be short (a few minutes) or long (45 minutes or more). This helps to avoid becoming distracted by the mind's desire and impulsivity to simply start doing other things.
3. Develop the habit of meditating in a certain spot and at a certain time of day. This helps train the mind to relax and to desire meditation.
4. Bring attention to your breathing, in particular your chest rising and falling with each breath.
5. Breathe normally and follow your breath with your attention. Just follow your breath moving in and out, and continue to breath normally.
6. When thoughts occur, which is normal, simply return attention back to the rising and falling of the breath, feeling the air coming into the chest and exhaling out.
7. Continue to meditate by following the breath despite any distractions that may occur including any thoughts,

sounds, and sensations. Just notice that your attention has wandered and gently bring it back to the breath. This is meditating. Keep doing this.

8. Meditate with your eyes slightly open; this helps to bring mindfulness into daily life. You can bring a meditative quality (mindfulness) to daily life by simply bringing attention to the breath whenever you remember. Set reminders and an intention to become aware of your breath whenever you hear the phone ring, your watch beeps, or you feel stress. Over time mediation will be recognized as your natural state.

Choiceless Awareness Meditation

1. Bring attention to the breath, or engage for a period of time in the Breath Awareness Meditation.

2. Instead of using the breath as the focus of meditation, change the focus of attention by observing arising phenomena in the sensory fields of sensation, sight, sound, taste, smell, and thoughts. Our attention is the steady witness.

3. Bring attention to a single sound or thought, or other arising phenomena. Watch the phenomena self-liberate, meaning fade into the unknown on its own. Repeat process.

4. If the mind gets lost in thought bring attention back to the sense field being specifically observed, or to the breath to stabilize attention.

5. Simply be attentive to whatever is arising. Whether sounds, sensations, thoughts, or even emotions, the only goal is not to get lost in the story or interpretation of what is arising.

6. By being a witness to the arising phenomena that come and go, impermanence can be observed. All things that come and go are no more than passing clouds in the clear

blue sky of Consciousness. This helps us to realize what is unchanging and permanent.

7. We discover the unchanging nature within us that stays unmoving no matter what is arising and passing away. This spacious awareness within us contains everything.

The Inner Witness

With a few techniques and trusting my own experiences, I was learning that all things were passing phenomena. This did not mean that I had lost interest in life. Meditation was helping me become more observant of what was going on around me, and a sense of spaciousness was growing within me. This spaciousness was helping me tune into the internal observer, or inner witness of my own feelings, body sensations, thoughts, and reactions. This inner witness was present during meditation sessions, during my work and personal life, including while I was talking with others. I found that I was more present to what was going on around me, with less energy directed at creating a story about things.

Life started taking on a richness that had not existed before. I was fully engaged in life, yet there was a surreal or dreamlike aspect about my daily routines and habits that I was finding easier to tap into. Events taking place around me were taking on a slow-motion quality. This was not because things were actually moving slower, but because there was a greater awareness of my own internal reactions or sense of presence. The fear of everyday existence and whether something unexpected or bad was going to happen was greatly diminished.

Self-Inquiry

Steve and I continued to feel fortunate that we found Joel, an enlightened teacher. In April, Steve and I met with him privately to introduce ourselves more personally and receive guidance regarding our meditation practices. This was also a requirement before attending one of the Center's retreats, which I was hoping to take part in soon. Since Steve and I were still new to the Center and were only attending public gatherings on Sundays, Joel did not know us very well. This is the journal entry I wrote at the time: "I explained that I had continued to do the self-inquiry 'Who am I?' meditation. Joel suggested that I back up as what I had taken on was the most direct, most profound question. He suggested that I inquire into thoughts (Who is thinking?), the body/sensations (Who is experiencing?), emotions (Who is feeling?), and also self-will (Who is doing?)."

I wish in hindsight that I had really taken in his suggestion. However, I believed I was already past that stage and what Joel was suggesting was only a beginner's practice, so I ended my journal entry with the following: "I have meditated on these questions already and I know them to lead back to the same place, but I still cannot find the Source. There is still only this emptiness and nothingness. The only way that I will experience that everything is included in this emptiness is to stick with the original question, 'Who am I?' If all is empty then emptiness must include everything."

Obviously, when I met Joel I needed a spiritual teacher who could slow me down, help me keep focused, and provide direct feedback to help me journey deeper. Unfortunately, trusting that a teacher could really understand and advise me correctly was difficult. I had become accustomed to figuring out things on my own. Yet Joel was a good teacher, patiently guiding his students and providing good examples of how to apply teachings to life's circumstances. It was only after walking further on the spiritual path that I could reflect on how helpful and direct Joel's advice had consistently been.

What follows is a description of the self-inquiry meditation practice, although there are many variations that can occur based on these introductory instructions. The following were helpful for me. I would eventually learn that as the spiritual practice deepens, so does the self-inquiry.

Self-Inquiry Practice (Who Am I?)

1. Bring mindfulness to what you are doing, either during formal meditation or simply by following the breath in daily life.

2. Be attentive to what you are feeling, or bring attention to the heart space by following the breath with attention.

3. Ask yourself, "Who am I?"

4. Feel the answer, since this is not something the mind can answer. Do not follow thoughts about who you are even if they are spiritual thoughts.

5. Feel who you are. Notice the unchanging stillness or presence within you. Rest your attention in this space.

6. Relax into the unknown space of the heart. This is where Truth is revealed.

7. To deepen the self-inquiry practice during formal meditation or in daily life ask the following questions: "Who is feeling? Who is thinking? Who is seeing? Who is doing? Who is experiencing?" And, even "Who is seeking?" Again, feel the answer in your heart.

Presence

After meeting with Joel, Steve and I went camping in the high desert of central Oregon. The sky was vast and the colorful canyons plentiful. We often meditated in the canyons or on mountains, then would walk back to our camper van in silence. I could stay in the present moment just being with what is for long periods. I also started observing how my mind liked to label experiences, especially wanting to call flashes of clarity "enlightenment."

In one meditation, I realized that I am already Self-realized. A new mantra spontaneously started, Being Consciousness Bliss. I focused on my heart center and breathing, just being with the mantra. There were no thoughts arising, just a clarity within me. I tried to distract myself by generating negative thoughts, any thoughts to test out my blank mind, then return to the mantra. Time and time again I would immediately come back to the Self, this vast presence. The mantra *Om Namo Bhagavate Sri Ramanaya* instantly reminded me to find the Self. I now knew from experience that the Self resides within the heart. In another meditation after focusing on my breath and heart center, I sensed a presence beyond anything I had known before. The canyon walls suddenly shimmered with splashes of light, as a gentle gust of wind met my breath. Time and my heart's boundaries disappeared. All was one and arising in this present moment. I knew I was the present moment arising. I wrote in my journal, "I believe this is some key breakthrough. However, it seems too simple."

Actually, in hindsight, I was onto something. The present moment is the only thing here. All of life is unfolding in this present moment. Truly, it is all there is. However, because this appears so obvious, as seekers it is easy to overlook. It just seems too simple.

> *...the Father's kingdom is spread upon the earth, and*
> *people do not see it.*
> *(The Gospel of Thomas, 200 AD)*[6]

PART II:

A Taste of Grace

Three

Dark Nights and Clear Light

*Surrender is beyond what the mind can do;
it is totally up to Grace.*

The Dark Night

In Spring 2003, I attended my first five-day meditation retreat at the Cloud Mountain Retreat Center.[7] Cloud Mountain is a beautiful retreat center on the side of a mountain in an old growth forest. It is located in Castle Rock, Washington. The surrounding nature avails itself to meditation, something I learned after attending several retreats. Witnessing the shifting light when the trees glisten in the filtered sun, the crisp air and the dampness showing the season changing, the colorful leaves falling then laying on the ground in various stages of decay, or new spring leaves dazzling as emeralds, all display the endless dance of impermanence. And one of my favorite sights, watching the wind bend the wispy trees into the trunks of neighboring trees, creating the sound of a haunting musical instrument.

It was not until this first retreat that all of my mantras stopped. Joel instructed us to follow our thoughts from their beginning to their natural conclusion, without getting lost in the story about them. When we do this, our thoughts fade away on their own, or self-liberate. To my surprise, when my mantra came up and I followed it to its conclusion, it stopped. No longer did my mantra dance in my mind. I could generate it by thinking about it, but it wasn't naturally flowing as it had been. At first it was unnerving. My mind had a blank quality to it much longer than I had ever experienced before. It wasn't returning to the mind's chatter or even my beloved mantra to Ramana. My mind was quiet, and my mantra was silent.

Soon after, Joel instructed us to drop any beliefs and fully be without a knowing mind. We were to select a belief we were attached to and let it go. Not knowing the consequences, I chose two beliefs that were closely tied to my spiritual understanding. The first was my belief in reincarnation. The second was my belief that there was a Ramana, a Divine Presence, a God. I fully let go into this unknowing. I returned to my room shaken. Unexpectedly, it sent my mind into a tailspin that led to my first spiritual crisis. I sat with my confusion for the greater part of twenty-four hours before I had finally felt that I had nothing to hold onto. If there were no God or Consciousness life was without meaning. I had no meaning or purpose. What was love then? I inquired deeper into this void of unknowing until I was exhausted.

I finally broke my silence and talked to one of the retreat leaders, Tom Kurzka.[8] The night before I was sleepless and grief-struck. I felt like I was ready to fall off the edge. The edge of *what* was the question. I was lost without knowing where to go or a direction to pursue. With copious tears and an anguished mind I needed reassurance that there was a God, that my connection to Ramana was true, and that there was a Consciousness, a divine loving energy that I felt inside me.

Tom, an awakened teacher himself, compassionately reassured me that there was. He also encouraged me that the next time I had such an experience of unknowing I should continue to venture into it even further. Tom said having this type of experience was a good sign that I was headed in the right direction. His suggestion was to not shut it off and to delve deep into the feelings of despair.

However, he cautioned that this is not something that can be forced and to allow it to come naturally. Once this feeling appears go as deep into the body sensations as possible. I could also slow down the experience just enough to peer at the story in the mind. "On the path you cannot take the little self with you, this is the process for letting go." Tom's final advice was to be like a warrior and surrender it all, including all preconceived notions and ideas of what constitutes reality, then leap off the cliff.

I later learned that many mystics describe such a journey as 'the dark night of the soul' or 'going through the spiritual desert.' The main advice is to not let the mind or fear get in the way of this deep exploration of the unknown. Despite leaving the retreat feeling that I had fallen short in making much spiritual progress, it inspired me to engage more fully in my meditation practice.

The Four Principles

Following the retreat I was also more motivated to learn about the teachings at the Center. Joel teaches the principles of Attention, Commitment, Detachment and Surrender. After studying each of the terms, I adapted them to my own practice and understanding. The importance of the first principle is to live with attention, that there is a unified Consciousness, which is revealed in this present moment. This is helped by focusing attention on the space within that does not change. The practice of attention is also applied so one is not swept away into sleep (laxity) when meditating. It can serve as the reminder to simply return to the breath, over and over, even as the mind in its endless chatter tries to distract us.

The second principle of Commitment is to live this spiritual life and hold awareness to this path no matter what is occurring. The commitment is constant, despite the inner and outer challenges, to continue the practice.

The third is the principle of Detachment to life events. This is experienced in our awareness of not grasping or pushing away life experiences, sensations, thoughts, or feelings. This does not mean that we do not love fully and with commitment. Instead, it means that there is a gentle awareness of the movement of impermanence within all these relationships, experiences, thoughts, feelings, and sensations. Detachment can also be practiced by not being seduced by elevated mind states (or bliss) or the mind's interpretations of so-called spiritual experiences.

Surrender means accepting that ultimately we are not in control. We only have the illusion of control to satisfy the ego, the mind. Surrender is a gentle relaxation and unconditional trust of the divine order of Consciousness, which we are all part of. This surrender means to live in acceptance of what is, to relax within oneself, as the grace of the Divine is revealed in its own time.

God Is in the Water

A few months after the retreat, Steve and I traveled to Nepal. This was a scheduled trekking vacation, but also turned into a journey to bring back a sacred, ceremonial crown for a Tibetan teacher. He was being honored for being a Rinpoche, a reincarnated being and great teacher from a previous life. Steve and I agreed that we would meet his uncle in Boudhanath to retrieve the crown and other gifts from his family.

Before arriving to Boudhanath, we spent a short time in zooming Kathmandu. It was a shock. We had imagined that all of Nepal would be like the photos we'd seen of the towering, yet serene Himalayas. Our journey from the airport to our motel was an adventure in trust. No seatbelts, or street lights for that matter. The air pollution and chaotic traffic, with all sizes of vehicles, the occasional cow and stray dog were all sharing the road, somehow avoiding each other at the last moment. Steve and I looked at each other with a silent smile, inside saying, "Oh my God!" We enjoyed visiting some Buddhist and Hindu Temples; many appeared unchanged since the Middle Ages.

Boudhanath is about four miles from Kathmandu. The towering Boudha Stupa, with the watchful eyes of the Buddha looking out in all four directions, was built sometime around 600 AD. The sound of little bells attached to the prayer flags fluttering in the wind, prayer wheels, the many Tibetan Buddhists engaged in their daily devotional rituals have remained locked in my memory. Meeting the teacher's uncle and sitting in his simple, humble room, I was intrigued by how important spirituality was in his life. Over half of his limited space housed a multi-layered altar.

We flew from Kathmandu to the quiet and peaceful town of Pokara. Against a backdrop of the Annapurna Mountains, it is also home to Nepal's second largest lake and a hub for the trekking scene, since most hikers need to travel through Pokara. As our time was limited, the next morning we waited for the wind to settle down, then flew through the narrow canyons of white-capped mountains. It was here in Jomsom that we connected with a guide and began our five-day trek.

Our trek took us deeper into the Kali Gandaki Valley, an area that follows one of the oldest rivers in the world, the Kali Gandaki. Fossils of marine animals have been found to date back over a million years. This area also includes the Himalayan Mountains of Annapurna and Dhaulagiri, and high desert region of the Tibetan plateau. Muktinath, a village our tour book mentions only in passing, would be our final destination before hiking back to Jomsom. We soon learned Muktinath is a sacred pilgrimage destination for Hindus and Buddhists. Often, we would come across pilgrims (monks, *sadhus* or ascetic holy men, and laypeople) many dressed in their best outfits or traditional attire of red, orange, yellow or white cloth. A few appeared to be honored holy men being led on horse or donkey by those walking on foot, as well as humble families making the pilgrimage together. After trekking through four villages along the way, and with breathtaking views of the Himalayas, we arrived.

The village of Muktinath is located at 12,300 feet, and the way of life has changed little through the centuries, except for the addition of some shops and guesthouses appealing to tourism. There is debate on how old Muktinath is, and how long pilgrims have been paying tribute. There is another Hindu temple closer to the Kali Gandaki River said to date back to 300-1000 AD. The Muktinath-Chuming Gyatsa Temple wasn't built until 1815. Whatever the facts, it is agreed that Muktinath has been and will continue to be a pilgrimage spot set like a gem on the Annapurna Circuit.

Slightly higher than the village, the temple grounds are at 12,467 feet. The entrance was lined with many temple bells, and once in the large courtyard our senses were greeted by the vibrant color and sounds of hundreds of prayer flags fluttering in the warm breeze. Trees thrive yet seem out of place considering the elevation. Small bells and chimes could be heard along with flowing water in the distance. We learned that part of Muktinath's spiritual appeal is that it has all four elements present: air, fire, water, and earth. Our first stop was the Tibetan Buddhist Temple. Within it was an underground eternal fire, which we were told has been burning for thousands of years. There were several large statues of Tibetan deities, the main one Chenrezig, and hundreds of small candles, many already flickering. Steve and I lit candles for our family, Joel, and Ramana.

We then visited the small Hindu shrine housing a sacred Golden Buddha, with many bells and statues of deities encircling it, and received a blessing from a Hindu priest. Steve later told me that the experience with the Buddha felt cosmic and powerful as if he had been mysteriously "zapped." Behind the shrine was a large courtyard, surrounded by 108 small, cow-head shaped waterspouts perched high on a wall of ancient stone. The pilgrims would touch the flowing water with their right hands then touch their heads, mouth, or heart (or all three). They worshiped each spout in the same manner. Some would pause at a certain spout in prayer, while others would hurry to visit each fountain repeatedly. There were two *sadhus* fully submerging themselves in the sacred pools, which were being filled by water flowing down from the cow-head fountains.

After watching for a while we joined behind a small line of *sadhus* who were approaching the first fountain. We joined in the ritual of touching the water from each spout, touching our right hands to our foreheads and finally our hearts. I started quietly singing a devotional mantra to Ramana as I offered gratitude at each fountain and the blessed water. About three-quarters of the way around I was filled with joy beyond words. Tears streamed down my face as I became one with the water. I realized that God was the water and that this was all a wonderful union with the Divine. I could go no farther as I fully experienced the rapture of this divine communion. It was then that I knew that nothingness did include everything. God was in the water. God was everything, which meant I was everything.

Three Sounds and No Silence

About four months later I was back at Cloud Mountain. The Center was offering a ten-day silent retreat, my longest. We were instructed to deepen the Choiceless Awareness meditation in order to discover what within us remained unchanged. By observing impermanence, what comes and goes, it would be easier for us to gain insights into the unchanging nature of Consciousness.

Cloud Mountain's beautiful grounds grant continuous opportunities to witness the play of sound, movement, and silence becoming One. Birds sing and call, the sound retreating into silence as they await their answer. All is enjoyed in each precious moment as there is nothing to hold onto and nothing lasts. Everything becomes an opportunity to witness how all of life is in a constant motion of change. All comes and goes in this beautiful dance, which is an endless revealing, a divine disclosure.

Studying sound would become my primary method for studying impermanence. As I strolled meditatively, I observed nature, especially paying attention to where sound came from and where I experienced it. Did I experience sound within or outside of myself?

I continued this practice over the next few days. While meditating in my room I heard the sound of a blue jay or raven cry out three calls. My mind stopped, but I suddenly realized that everything arises in and returns to Consciousness. All is Consciousness no matter the movement. Just as sounds arise and return to Consciousness, I knew there to be no death, truly no impermanence in the mind's understanding of it. The meditative state then deepened beyond anything I had ever experienced.

There was an intense buzzing in my ears and I did not seem to have control of my body. It was as though everything stopped, then started with this renewed freshness. I was suddenly fully alive in awareness, yet I was doing nothing. The presence of myself was the presence of everything. I was beyond my body and its limitations. My eyes felt like they were forced shut, as I could see nothing but a bluish clear light. I do not know how long I was there. The experience was beyond bliss. Then my body seemed to be released and I could move again. When I opened my eyes I felt tears, then pried my fingers apart and unfolded my legs. Everything seemed to be happening in slow motion, and seemed timeless. I gradually looked around the room hearing the piercing sounds of nature outside. The colors of the trees blowing were brilliant. No thoughts were arising, just the awareness of my surroundings. I was in awe of the naturalness of all arising.

Gradually, I returned to the thinking mind as I tried to understand what had happened and wondered if this was enlightenment. That night, I experienced becoming lucid while dreaming. I experienced the same bluish light and a profound sense of peace. There was no bodily awareness and I felt absolutely free from everything. There was only the presence of eternal peace and a vast spaciousness. There were no boundaries, no fear, no thoughts, no yearning for anything. I was home in this silent comfort. I thought of never wanting to leave this space, and then awoke.

I later learned that this was the experience of dreamless sleep. With the sense of a newfound awareness I went to see Joel. I could only imagine my experience was enlightenment or gnosis (absolute knowing) or at least a gnostic flash (as Joel had described). He advised me not to label the experience, as the mind in its grasping will try to own the experience. Once the mind takes ownership, it simply is relegated to something from the past. He explained that the mind tends to be frightened of change, of being disregarded, so he told me not to be afraid of "don't know mind." Thus, it's important not to cling to the experience and try to decipher it.

If it is gnosis or enlightenment then it is here to stay. However, if it is a gnostic 'flash' it will pass, but it is to be accepted as a gift from Grace and I should learn from it. Joel explained that the principles of attention and commitment had moved me to this stage, now it was time to practice detachment and surrender. He stressed surrender is not something the mind can do, it is totally up to Grace.

Facing the Void

After the retreat ended, I gradually returned to my householder's life. The glow of the retreat would gradually fade. However, for several weeks I believed I must have awakened because of the clarity and spaciousness I felt. I would return and return to this space during my busy life or when life became challenging. Emotions of irritation and impatience seemed to arise in slow motion, as I was residing more as the witness of the experiences going on around me.

Still, this was not enough. I became nearly obsessed with wanting to return to the state I had experienced during the retreat. I didn't understand what had happened, but only knew I no longer feared death. The dreamless sleep experience showed me that the passage to Consciousness was within me. I talked to Joel again and asked his advice. He recommended that I study Tibetan Dream Yoga,[9] since what I experienced was likely a clear light experience. After reading more on the subject, I learned that a clear light experience was glimpsing the radiant mind, a subtle mind state that happens during death or during the end stage of advanced tantric practice. I started studying to increase my night practice.

For a few weeks following the retreat, I tried in vain to repeat the clear light and dreamless sleep experience. It seemed the more I tried to become lucid, that I couldn't achieve it. This was another lesson in understanding Grace. I learned that things happen on their own, and that the experiences I had were because of Grace, not me. Soon after I stopped trying, I had another clear light experience. This time I became lucid as I was falling down a tunnel of light. I passed through white, then gray, black, to gray again. It was the same experience of emptiness and the incredible sense of peace I experienced during the retreat. I wondered if I was traveling through the bardo, noted in Tibetan Buddhist teachings as the stages of consciousness one passes through, including when leaving the body. There was another thought, "I must be dying." Then another thought countered that it was not yet time. I woke up soon after.

My dreamless sleep experiences were few from that point on, but there was still this intense yearning to merge with the Divine, with Ramana, with God. The devotion I was feeling was so powerful my heart ached. I wanted union. I did not care if I died and, paradoxically, I was no longer afraid to live. I believed I had glimpsed the other side and could not deny this knowing.

I went to talk to Joel again.

Joel explained that while my clear light practice and meditations were coming along nicely, I should be aware that anything arising from the mind is just that. If there is a narration about a particular experience, it is the mind working. He told me not to listen to it. Occasionally, the mind can echo an insight that can be helpful, but generally all thoughts arising should be ignored. I described a meditation in which I experienced the wind, the mantra, and God all being the same.

Joel said that on a positive note this showed that my meditations were deepening and that I was becoming an advanced meditator, which tasted like temporary candy for my ego. He then cautioned about seeking to repeat experiences and the danger of allowing the mind to create a story about them. Seeing the experiences and insights as gifts of Grace was important, yet to stay neutral and present with what is arising.

Despite this advice, I was not ready to follow it. Everything I was trying to recreate was just more grasping at past experiences. Yet I convinced myself that the dreamless sleep and deep meditative states I had during the retreat were somehow different. I believed I had glimpsed Consciousness itself, and glimpsing God certainly must be the exception to the rule since this leads to enlightenment. At the time, I believed I was on the right track. The possibility that I had tasted Truth was not something I wanted to ignore.

However, by all my waiting and grasping for the big realization to occur, I continued to hold onto the memories of my mind states. It was a subtle distraction that kept me from searching beyond what I had previously experienced or knew intellectually. This prevented me from looking for what was just beneath the surface. Namely, who was the experiencer of these spiritual insights and heightened mind states, and where was the source of these experiences?

The Calling

Nonetheless, I felt a strong calling to travel to India a few months after the Fall Retreat. I envisioned traveling alone to fully be present with the impermanence of life around me. Varanasi, the 3,000 year old city located on the northern planes of the Ganges would be my main destination. Considered one of the oldest cities in the world, over a million spiritual pilgrims visit each year. Bathing in the Holy River Ganges is said to release sin, while dying and being cremated here is said to bring liberation.

I wanted to meditate at the burning *ghats* where I could witness death and the sacred cremations firsthand. I believed by doing so it would help me find the Truth. I would gain insight into my own mortality, thus, my own spiritual essence. From there, I planned to visit Bodhgaya, where the Buddha Shakyamuni became enlightened. Finally, the journey would end at Ramana's sacred mountain, Arunachala.[10] Traveling to Arunachala and visiting Ramana's ashram would be a pilgrimage of devotion.

I prayed for guidance since this trip was still tied to my yearning to merge with the Divine. I still felt ready to accept whatever there was, even death. I surrendered, knowing that God would show me the way to my deepest Self, and believed this would happen if I was prepared to journey with an open heart into the unknown, come what be. The spiritual pursuit had become the most important thing in my life. I felt I had touched Presence, and wanted to lose myself once more in the light of this recognition.

Four

Personal Retreats

*No matter where we are or what may be happening,
connecting with the Self, our True Nature, is readily
available as the in-breath.*

S teve and I were now going to the Center regularly, attending
both a study group and Sunday gatherings. We also looked
forward to attending the offered retreats. In fact, I found the retreat
experiences addicting. I wanted more experiences, more insights. I
was motivated to find more opportunities for retreats, beyond just
the few times of year offered through the Center. I researched other
retreats, which were often expensive. Soon, I discovered I could
create my own retreat at home or when we would camp. I developed
some structure to get the most out of my time, which included
making retreat vows and following some basic precepts of behavior
similar to those at the Center retreats.

As I grew more accustomed to personal or solo retreats, I
decided I could also bring increased mindfulness into my fast-paced,
working world. This inspired me to create a structured retreat that I
could carry out while I was working at my job. Before going into the
details on the structure and how I conducted retreats while living a
householder's life, it is timely to describe a few more practices from

the Center, in particular the precept practice and the renunciate vows taken on retreat.

Precepts and Retreat Vows from Center

The Ten Selfless Precepts from the Center for Sacred Sciences are recited during retreat, as well as during study groups. Members are encouraged to weave these precepts into their daily life, and see what comes of them. Often the first precept of Responsibility is a powerful place to start, since it helps to activate the inner witness, encouraging us to observe how we are reacting to life as it unfolds around us. The meaning of each precept can deepen over time. Members will often focus on one precept for a while to see how it operates in their lives. The precepts are eventually memorized, and are repeated daily to obtain the most benefit. I practiced these for years, and found them helpful to become aware of my conditioned behaviors, especially reactive patterns and ego-driven desires. The following Ten Selfless Precepts, and the Renunciate Vows otherwise known as retreat vows, are recited as follows:

I Vow to Practice these TEN SELFLESS PRECEPTS

1. **Responsibility**. To take responsibility for my life. Not to blame others for my own unhappiness, nor make excuses for my own mistakes.

2. **Self-Discipline**. To regard each moment as a precious opportunity for spiritual practice. Not to waste time in frivolous pursuits, nor overindulge in drugs, alcohol, or escapist entertainments.

3. **Harmlessness**. Not to injure or kill any being heedlessly or needlessly.

4. **Stewardship**. Not to waste the resources upon which other beings depend.

5. **Honesty**. Not to deceive myself, or others by word or deed.

6. **Integrity**. Not to take what does not belong to me.

7. **Honor**. To regard my word as sacred, not to give it lightly but once given, strive to honor it under all circumstances.

8. **Sexual Restraint**. To make of sex a sacrament, not to profane it in the pursuit of selfish ends.

9. **Charity**. Not to be possessive of people or things, but to give unsparingly of my assets, both material and spiritual, for the alleviation of suffering.

10. **Remembrance**. To recite these precepts once a day, renewing my vows and remembering this path which I have freely chosen.

Renunciate Vows (Retreat Vows), Center For Sacred Sciences

1. To practice **poverty** by realizing that, in reality, nothing belongs to me.

2. To practice **chastity** by refraining from all sexual behavior, and from indulging in sexual fantasies.

3. To practice strict **obedience** to all my precepts, as well as to the rules of this retreat center.

4. To maintain **outer silence**, except for speech related to teachings and tasks; and to allow **inner silence** to permeate my heart and mind.

5. To strive for **constancy** in my practice, both day and night.

Creating Retreats

Because my first solo retreats were either at home or with my husband, breaking silence in the evening seemed natural, especially while camping and needing to discuss some kind of practical household business. I rarely had the luxury of having the house to myself, so I adapted my retreats to fit my environment. Fortunately, Steve was supportive and did his best to decrease the noise and demands placed on me such as answering the phone, running errands, and cooking.

During home retreats, I set up our spare room as my meditation and private sleeping area. I would cover the television with a large cloth and set up an altar in front of it. I resolved to meditate a certain number of hours a day mixed with listening to meditation tapes or watching videos, journal writing, mindful walking, and even napping. Eating lightly during these retreats also helped to deepen the meditation experience and decrease sleepiness. I practiced Tibetan dream yoga by being as mindful as possible as I fell asleep, then I logged my dreams in my journal.

Meditations were a mixture of concentration (breath practice), mantra practice, self-inquiry, and choiceless awareness. Simply resting in spacious awareness was the primary goal. Here is a journal entry about my first five-day home retreat: "January 21. It's 10:39 p.m. and I will begin my silent retreat. My focus will be to study impermanence by watching my thoughts, experiences, and witnessing this in nature. I have some spiritual tapes and CD's from Joel's teachings, as well as from Joseph Goldstein. I will take the ten precepts from the Center as well as the retreat vows. I will also add on a few rules for myself to enhance the structure of the retreat."

Structure for Home Silent Retreats

1. To be mindful of my thoughts.

2. To be mindful of my breath.

3. To be mindful as I fall asleep and also during dreaming.

4. To not over-indulge in sleeping.

5. To keep a schedule, and meditate at least three hours daily.

6. To be mindful during teachings.

7. To complete chores and household duties for the benefit of those I live with and care for.

8. To practice yoga or other exercise for my body daily.

9. To pay attention to any grasping onto experiences, especially being mindful that my interpretation of reality is only a thought about it. Allow experiences to be experiences.

10. To eat lightly or moderately, to avoid over-indulgences.

During my retreats or spiritual quests while camping with Steve, we would begin our day together then separate for several hours going our own way. Central and eastern Oregon are ideal locations for retreats since they offer many secluded places, grand vistas, and a big sky. During these retreats, I would often find a sprawling juniper tree and sit under it for hours. I would set up my altar, bring my journal, and be present to whatever would arise. I worked hard at not striving for experiences. Gradually, a trust was building that things would happen in their own time and perfection.

Finally, I also started taking "Working Retreats" as I called them. The longest of these was for eight days. I would continue going to my job and interacting with the world, along with creating a structured practice while at home, and keeping retreat vows. A short journal entry clarified the purpose of the first working retreat, "February 29. My goal is to enhance mindfulness in all of my daily activities, including home and work-related tasks in order to create greater awareness of spaciousness and being a witness to phenomena arising and passing."

The following is the structure and my retreat vows:

Structure and Retreat Rules for Working Retreat

1. Repeat retreat vows from the Center, as well as abide by the 10 Selfless Precepts.

2. To engage in speech that is compassionate and beneficial to others despite my taking a vow of silence.

3. To allow inner silence to permeate my heart and mind.

4. To refrain from sweets or other compulsive eating, realizing that all efforts to satisfy my body will be endless.

5. To meditate at least 2 hours daily on work days, 3 hours daily on non-work days.

6. To build in yoga, walking meditation or physical activity daily.

7. To be keenly aware of all of my interactions so that mindfulness can increase spontaneously.

8. To not cling to, nor avoid bliss or other altered states during meditation.

9. To especially practice compassion and humility during this week.

10. To not break this retreat, no matter how challenging, boring, or uneventful it may seem.

Over the next four months, I engaged in some type of retreat at least once a month. The following journal entries described some of my experiences: "Meditated on there being no mind. Each time I would find myself engaged in thought (even spiritual thoughts), I would focus on the heart center. I would guard my mind, trying to catch any thought arising, so I would not get lost in it. Sometimes I would succeed, other times not, but the sense of spaciousness only seems to be deepening." During another retreat I wrote, "There have been several dreams about ice. The message seems clear. It is time to 'thaw the ice' by going directly into the heart when I feel resistance to a person or situation. The ice is delusion, which will melt in the water of pure awareness when recognized."

Finally, in another retreat I experienced a breakthrough while inquiring into who is hearing, who is feeling, and who is sensing? My journal continued, "All self-liberates and returns to the Source. It is the bottomless ground, the conscious awareness of all existence, the simplicity of the present moment. It is the no-thing of absolute potentiality. This explains why Emptiness creates the space for all to manifest. An open void, a receptive vessel without boundaries, this is what we are. It is all here now, and can only be. Let me remember this without the mind stepping in."

After completing my first working retreat, I noted the following impressions: "You can take mindfulness into any situation; you don't have to be quiet to experience an inner state of peace. It is always here. And this 'I' is like breathing into the heart center. It is as readily available as the in-breath."

I scheduled another meeting with Joel to ask questions about my meditations. I described how my eyes sometimes felt like they were glued shut. Soon after this sensation, there would be a ringing or buzzing in my ears, and the appearance of a bluish-white space overtaking my visual field. After fifteen or twenty minutes, the experience would vanish as though I was released by the intense presence of whatever was mysteriously holding me.

Joel suggested I research *samadhi* states. He also cautioned once again to avoid clinging or grasping, as well as not pushing away what is arising. I explained that while trying to practice detachment, I was now trying to avoid bliss states, since bliss states seemed to arise too easily and were distracting. I explained how I was now only striving to remain steady by not becoming seduced by the heightened bliss experiences. Joel explained the problem with these types of endeavors. It seems that avoiding what is happening is the same as clinging to an experience. He advised me to simply allow bliss and other sensations to come and go without pushing them away or trying for a different experience. I was to remain a steady witness to phenomena arising: Just watch, feel whatever is passing through, and let it go.

Divine Order

I attended the Center's annual Spring Retreat at Cloud Mountain in April. I was planning to buy my ticket to India when I returned. While walking in the woods, attuning to the sounds of nature, I suddenly knew everything to be in divine order. The words, "Being Consciousness Bliss" intuitively came to me in a mysterious meeting with an imposing maple tree. Moss coated its branches, and as I looked up I became lost in a sea of green layers. I instantly recognized how everything in the present moment is Consciousness. The extraordinary tree could only be experienced in the now, within me. All became vividly clear. Being only happens in the present moment. Consciousness is this Presence, and Bliss is only experienced in present-moment awareness. The tree was inside of me. Each breath was this Presence, and this is who I was. Paradoxically, any sense of past and future thinking still only existed in the Now. Even my spiritual yearning was taking place in the presence of who I was. Suddenly, I laughed. I knew I was never separate from the Divine and did not need to go to India. There was nowhere to go, and nothing to die into. Ramana and the Divine were within me. The sense of wanting to die into the Mystery ended on that day.

Journey into the Whale

When I returned home from the retreat, I cancelled my trip and informed my supervisor of my decision since I had requested a month off from work. I also contacted the Ramana Maharshi Ashram, where I had been planning to stay. People around me voiced surprise about my canceling my plans. However, when I recall a dream just before the retreat, my subconscious seemed to know something I did not. The dream started with me walking along a trail near our house. Ahead I spotted several wandering *sadhus* (ascetic holy men) all scantily dressed in colorful orange cloth. I joined them but soon found myself walking alone. In the dream I had no supplies or water, but I knew I was embarking on a journey to India. I then sensed that dark was falling so I started running. Soon I was racing along as I dodged rocks on the trail.

The trail led into a small canyon of two walls of smooth stone. I was forced to squeeze through the space as it started to narrow. After realizing I was dreaming I remained lucid. I placed my hands on the stone walls and said, "May these stones hold solid if it is meant for me to go to India." The walls opened slightly then transformed into an enormous, fossilized whale tail. I entered the whale through its tail, as if it were the entrance to a cave.

I could see the details of colossal ribs above me and felt the damp coolness inside this giant being. I continued out through its mouth and now ended up in a second whale, this time entering through its mouth. I reached the center of the second whale and it seemed that I was supposed to lie down. I lay down on the cold ground of the whale and was fully present, feeling my breath and a tantric sensation rising up and passing through my body. All at once, the whale was filled with rainbow light everywhere, filling me with ecstasy beyond anything I'd ever experienced before. I felt as though I had left my body and was the rainbow light that was everywhere within the whale. After a while, I rose and returned home telling Steve I would go to India someday but would be better prepared. When I awoke the next morning, I remembered the dream, but did not understand what it meant. Following the retreat, it seemed Mother India had eluded me once again, but I was okay with it. I felt at peace.

Five

The Heart and a Glimpse of Truth

What we feel emotionally and spiritually is subjectively sensed within the space of our own hearts. Gradually, the perception of the world begins to grow larger, as the heart expands to sense all of life through its increasing presence.

The Opening

Following the retreat, I felt more balanced about how to develop spiritually. I was still committed, but wasn't so intensely driven. I was working full-time at the hospital, often at a frenzied pace, and aspired to draw from my spiritual well during times of stress. I was also a wife, and a part-time stepparent to a 14 year old. I was engaged in a regular meditation practice, though the drive to penetrate the boundaries of my own mortality and the Divine's was put to rest.

Developing more of an understanding about self-inquiry, I continued my meditation practice for the next several months. Self-inquiry, as Ramana Maharshi taught was for devotees to ask themselves the question, "Who Am I?" Paradoxically, this is not a question that the mind can answer (as I learned after doing it incorrectly for the first several months). The purpose, rather than following thoughts, is to feel or sense the answer. After all, thoughts come and go. One can witness this by paying attention to the origin and passing of any thought. Most thoughts and feelings are rarely connected to what is happening in the present moment. So by asking the question "Who Am I?" without allowing mental responses to fill this space of unknowing, there is simply a return to our natural being which is spaciousness, the space within that does not change.

At first the experiences of spaciousness were fleeting, as it seemed too obvious, too simple. I would grow bored and instead try to conjure an image or profound insight. However, I was beginning to learn more about my own mind through this process. It was so tempting to follow any spiritual experience or insight to the point that I'd be distracted from simply resting in stillness. Using my self-inquiry practice, I discovered that the mind with its creative answers and quick adaptation to questions would continually compile ever more intriguing answers and experiences which seemed designed to steal my attention. I learned slowly over time that my mind was not to be trusted, nor was it able to understand the question to begin with. The mind also could not own these experiential glimpses into Awareness since they were beyond thought. Knowing that the answer was not to be found in my thoughts, dipping into the space of inner stillness was becoming easier for me. Nonetheless, *residing* in the silence of spaciousness was a continual challenge.

After a few more months into the self-inquiry practice, a deeper understanding into the question of "Who Am I?" was developing. By the summer of 2004 I was experiencing spacious awareness while not meditating. Soon after this discovery, I met another awakened teacher, David Waldman.[11] With strong connections to Ramana Maharshi and the sacred mountain Arunachala in southern India, he teaches the path of *Advaita Vedanta*, or the non-dual teachings.

Much had happened in my life just before my first meeting with David. In July, in an unexpected series of events, my maternal grandmother and my father died within six days of each other. I first flew to Minnesota to be at my grandmother's bedside, joining my five siblings. Due to our age differences and strained family relationships, this was the first time we had all been together. It was an incredibly moving memorial service and the first time I had seen my grandfather cry. My family was able to laugh while sharing funny stories, as well as to express our grief, which was a new experience for us. Despite this emotional time, I noticed that the spaciousness within my heart was still with me. It was the unchanging space within me to which I was beginning to return.

Soon after returning to Oregon, I was notified of my father's unexpected death. I would later learn that he committed suicide. He had been living a lonely life in southern Oregon after becoming alienated from most family members. Two of my sisters arrived to help me deal with his affairs, and soon I returned to Minnesota with his ashes so he could be near his family, as he had wished. Our family arranged another memorial service. It was again an open expression of grief, funny stories, and a time for each of us to describe our relationship with him, and to identify the strengths we had gained. By taking part in these testimonials I recognized that a deep healing was taking place, not just for me but also for my whole family. Interestingly, the more I opened and revealed myself, I noticed that my family members did the same. They also talked from their hearts, not the typical avoiding or blocking emotions I had come to expect when we gathered as a family. It was as though my family perfectly mirrored the openness that I felt inside; the walls of protection were coming down. What came first I do not know.

Despite the challenging relationship I had with my father, I allowed the grief simply to be there. I allowed myself to tap into the love I felt for my dad despite his mental illness and years of addiction. My heart felt even more expansive, which I attributed to my willingness to be present and fully feel my emotions. I recognized that my grandmother and father's deaths did not remove their presence, which remained fully intact within me. Now, the spaciousness within also included them, along with an awareness that there was no inside or outside, and no death. But most importantly, through these deaths, I felt a growing capacity to feel and express love.

After returning home, I admit I felt emotionally exhausted. Needing some downtime, I gave in to watching television and mindlessly channel surfing. I landed on a public broadcast channel. A full-screen photo of Ramana Maharshi's face appeared. At first I imagined that I was having a vision. The "vision" quickly ended and turned out to be some sort of *satsang*. I listened to the speaker, immediately resonating with his words. Beside him was a photo of Ramana Maharshi. Since I hadn't heard the speaker's name, I planned to ask at the Center to see if anyone had watched the broadcast.

Two days later, I watched a video a friend from the Center had recommended. She deliberately held back the details only saying I needed to watch it. To my awe the video began with the same large picture of Ramana's face. I learned David was a teacher giving *satsangs* in Portland, a two-hour drive from Eugene. After watching the video I found his website, and learned all I could about him and his teachings. Within a few days I connected with two women who were driving to Portland for a *satsang* with him later in the week. It felt that everything was so well scripted for my first meeting with David. Less than a week after first watching the broadcast, I simply introduced myself by saying, "Ramana sent me."

Beyond Mind States

Shortly after this meeting, Joel had us choose a spiritual book to read contemplatively. Primed to deepen my self-inquiry practice, I chose *The Spiritual Teachings of Ramana Maharshi*.[12] Soon after, I started experiencing *samadhi* states that varied in intensity. Describing a *samadhi* state is difficult, as there are different levels of this mind state, and depending on whether we perceive ourselves as a separate witness to the experience; or, are one with the experience, the level of insight potentially gained during a *samadhi* state will vary. It is unlike most experiences during meditation, where there is the constant roping in of the mind as thoughts, images, and sensations come and go.

A deep *samadhi* is a state of unified consciousness. This means that there is not a separate experiencer in *samadhi*, as all is arising in Consciousness, including even the experiencer, namely us. A *samadhi* can also occur in which all thoughts stop, however there is still a subtle sense of being a separate self, experiencing the deep mind state arising. Sometimes a physical vibration or a direct sinking into a sense of nothingness is experienced, as in an abyss or void, which has been my experience on several occasions.

However, dropping into a *samadhi* state is just that, a state, which means that it is something that will pass. I could sometimes glimpse or carry over my sense of being one with Consciousness, but couldn't hold onto this once I returned to my spiritual quest, otherwise known as the life of a seeker.

At first there was always a ringing in my ears, and a bluish light would appear, though this was changing. The *samadhi* states would happen without warning and were happening more often, sometimes even while driving or at work, and they were not lasting as long as previously. These spontaneous states were happening several times weekly, holding me in vivid stillness for several seconds or minutes at a time. They were blissful, yet somehow felt natural. The bliss was mysteriously my own awareness. I was awake, ever aware of the present moment. The sense of self versus other, or inside versus outside, were beginning to merge along with a growing sense that there was only One.

Strangely, as I read passages from Ramana's book or while meditating, my neck and head would also start moving slowly side to side. Yet, the rest of my body felt unmovable, as if weighted down. I seemed to be returning to a vast inner spaciousness without boundaries. By fall, my self-inquiry practice was deepening and a noticeable perception of awareness permeated my life. I was sensing life like never before.

My perception of the world was expanding, and my heart was now sensing all of life through its growing presence. However, even with the *samadhi* states and the insights of unity when real life came flooding back in, I—with my ego-driven conditioning and sense of separateness—was still present as ever. Bringing the mindfulness to my work life was especially challenging. Therefore, I started to study myself while at work. I watched how anxiety or impatience would arise then recede like waves. Or feelings of stress would come and go, as would joy.

During this time, I wrote in my journal: "I am learning that mind states, along with our bodily sensations and emotional flurries, will always pass. They continually transform into another state or experience. It is to discover what within us remains unchanged. Then, Consciousness, the true Self is revealed."

Realizing the Self

I attended my second weekend retreat with David in November. Despite the heart opening, I believed there were some areas in my life I was holding back. In talking to David, I revealed that despite many experiences of spaciousness and unity, I could still sense subtle, protective walls that kept me from being fully open and trusting. David explained that for some spiritual seekers relationships with people are more difficult, while a relationship with the unmanifested, the Mystery, comes easier. He believed this was true for me. I could feel the truth of his words. It was so much easier for me to meditate, slip into altered states, and to have a relationship with the Divine. Dealing with people and life around me, on the other hand, seemed more challenging. After this disclosure, the openness within me felt more expansive. It seemed another protective shield around my heart was lifted by simply acknowledging it.

The retreat was offered in Eugene, so I'd return home between sessions, where I had set up our spare room to continue the retreat. I slowly read passages from the Ramana book to feel the words penetrate my heart. When I returned to the retreat the second day, some new self-inquiry questions emerged. "What is the source of attention?" I asked. In following attention back to its source, I found it to originate and return to the same place. The source of attention came and returned from the heart, not the mind.

I allowed my attention to be within my heart without following any thoughts or trying to analyze it. I experienced a deep relaxation into the heart space. The second question came soon after, "Where is the source of bliss?" Again, it originated from within me (the heart) and returned into me. The third question and most powerful was, "Where is the source of other?" In my experience of myself, the Self (the unchanging presence within) revealed there to be only one Source. The person sitting in front, behind, and beside me were all from the same Source. Within the sense of the heart, there were no boundaries.

Inquiring deeper, "What is the source of self?" was the next question. The source of self, my identity, originated from my own heart. I knew this source to be Awareness, Consciousness. A grand experience of spaciousness and bliss overcame me, but I returned to the inquiry. I asked, "What is the source of thoughts?" Again it was the same answer. I asked, "What is the source of other?" This time, I found there was no other besides the experience of myself. The inquiry continued with sounds, sights, everything that I could see and experience. There was a return to the first question, "Where does attention arise?" Finally, I completed the self-inquiry by asking, "Who am I?" I immediately knew there to be only One. There is only the Self. *I* was the Self. I knew the Self to be the spaciousness without the self-imposed limits of the mind. I knew that I had realized the Self.

Doubting Mind

Following the retreat, it seemed the experience of realizing the Self was here to stay. It was the space I woke up to and abided in throughout the day. There was only the space within that never changes. It was a knowledge that was beyond the mind and resided in the heart. About a month later, a friend and I talked about our spiritual progress. She had once made me promise to tell her if I ever had a spiritual breakthrough. She agreed to do the same. Remembering this, I gingerly revealed my Self-realization. I immediately felt awkward. I went home and wrote the following in my journal: "I felt she doubted me, but the experience of awareness is the experience of awareness. What more can there be? It did trigger doubt in me, but I know this is only the mind, just thoughts. I remember something that Tom Kurzka once said, 'The mind has no authority over the Self.'" This seemed to ease my mind, at least for a while.

The Source

While some lingering doubts remained, my spiritual thirst became even stronger. I wondered if there was more to discover, and if I had merely penetrated the first layers of realization. While I knew I had realized the Self, I wondered if there was a source beyond this recognition. I decided to explore this question further by means of self-inquiry, and increasing my meditation to at least ten hours weekly. I meditated on the source, to find the source of the Self, the source of the 'I' experienced as my own awareness.

After calming my mind by simply following the breath, I rested in meditative spaciousness. I began the self-inquiry, 'Where is the source of Self?' Focusing intensely on the heart space, I waited. With attention looking inward, my mind was blank. I knew the answer would be known through direct experience. After doing this practice several times, the spaciousness of my heart space revealed the answer. The boundaries of space merged to include my inner perceptions and what was perceived outside of my body. The source was shown to be the whole of my experience. I knew the source was the Self. All is the wondrous, limited space of Presence, our very own awareness.

Soon after I began meditating on the Source, an unexpected calling came to light. Until this time, I was fully content with not traveling to India. To the surprise of my husband, and myself, I announced that I wanted to go to India as soon as possible. Within a few days I had my itinerary and was awaiting my tourist VISA for a pilgrimage to honor my heart guru, Ramana Maharshi. I planned to visit his ashram, and walk on his beloved mountain, Arunachala. The dates coincided with part of David's retreat in Tiruvannamalai that I also planned to attend.

I went to see Joel for spiritual advice. In all honesty, I needed his validation of my perceived awakening. I filled in Joel on my experiences of awareness. I struggled with what to call it, since enlightenment didn't really seem to describe it as much as the realization of the Self. Joel advised me not to become attached or to label experiences, nor to cling to the belief that experiences now had to be a certain way. He reminded me that all is unfolding in Consciousness. He explained that this is why he likes the description of enlightenment as freedom.

Dreams before India

Before my sudden plans to travel to India, I dreamt that an unidentified man was talking to me. He told me there was no difference between what is seen outside and what is perceived inside and elaborated that there is no separation. Another dream was about Joel. He gave me a book on non-dual teachings. The cover of the book had the word Arunachala and a picture of the Mountain. I became emotional in my dream and overcome by the bliss of understanding.

Cup too Full

Joel once told a story about a Zen student who went to his teacher requesting a teaching. The Zen master then asks the student if he would like some tea, which the student happily accepts. The teacher keeps pouring until the tea pours over the sides of the teacup and onto the floor. The student becomes disturbed by this seemingly absentminded act of his teacher, asking the teacher to explain his actions. The teacher simply responds that there was no teaching to give the student because his cup was already too full. Before my trip to India, I must admit this student was me. I had developed a case of spiritual pride and would not realize it until much later.

Before leaving for India, I drove to Portland to attend a weekend retreat given by David. After his monologue, my heart started pounding so hard I felt compelled to sit with him. We just sat there looking at each other. No words were spoken; no teachings were offered. I guessed that perhaps this was David's way of quietly validating my spiritual progress. We ended our time together with a Namaste greeting. I then said, "And, hello *Sangha*." I had not attended a *satsang* since the last retreat a few months earlier. I believed I had completed my spiritual work with David and it was time to continue the deeper spiritual unfolding on my own. Yet, now I was joining seventeen *sangha* members on a retreat in India. It only felt right to reach out and make contact again.

When David and I were talking privately I joked, "I thought it was best that I came out of my shell." David looked in my eyes and without pausing said, "There is only going inside, not going outside." I immediately remembered my recent dream. This caught me off guard, but I answered quickly and confidently, "Oh, I know that." David looked at me deeply and said either he was not so sure or his look alone gave me that message.

Another meeting with David the next day was more validating for my ego. However, in hindsight I still had a long way to go on the Heart's path. I sat with him following a monologue he gave on having a willingness to place your attention toward the Divine. In this willingness to be with the Mystery, there is a letting go, the action of doing (effort) stops because we trust that our lives are guided, and we relax knowing all is happening as it is meant to be. I said that I had come to sit in willingness. David asked me what it was that I wanted. I said, "Nothing." He said he had nothing to offer me that I did not already have, that we were the same.

David reminded me of how I used to talk with him, saying that now my face was open and bright. He talked about how I took a break from him to find the teacher within, saying this is where all my answers reside, that he could only direct me back within. He looked directly into my eyes. David said many layers of my ego had subsided or vanished, saying again all I needed to do was go within. David's final monologue was about the difference between Self-realization and freedom. He described Self-realization as the first step until there is a further deepening into the Self beyond ego-attachments, which leads to freedom.

During the retreat, I was mysteriously attracted to a Dancing Shiva statue on the altar. I had seen the statue before, but never particularly noticed it. I knew Shiva represented the divine energy of fire. I started to imagine this fire burning through the remaining layers of my ego and any resistance. Breathing into the heart space, I visualized Shiva dancing within the heart, the flame of liberation penetrating my being. Burning away everything, allowing the fire to be felt within my heart was my meditation. I continued this meditation through the day and into the night. I watched how thoughts and body sensations arose on their own. There truly is no doer. Sensations and actions arise and pass away on their own. It is all just this dance.

I ended the retreat with a full heart and sensed that I'd somehow formed a relationship with Shiva. David and I hugged since I felt a greater welcoming toward him as my teacher. We would soon connect in India. His group would leave in a few days, and I would travel alone through Singapore, joining them later in the week. I knew this would be a journey into the heart. However, I had the feeling I was simply to show up and allow Grace to do the rest.

PART III:

The Deepening

Six

Journey to the Mountain

*Arunachala! Thou dost root out the ego of those who
meditate on thee in the heart.*[13]
~Bhagavan Sri Ramana Maharshi

Despite telling myself I was traveling empty-handed, I still had
notions about India and what this retreat would mean to me
spiritually. I anticipated spending most of my time meditating,
deepening my self-inquiry practice and simply basking in the
Source. Since this trip was in honor of Ramana Maharshi, I planned
to visit his ashram often.

The Mystery seemed to have other plans. It was not until
arriving in Tiruvannamalai that I felt the intense pull of the
mountain Arunachala. Hindus believe Arunachala embodies Shiva;
thus, it has been an important pilgrimage destination for over a
thousand years. At 1,600 feet, this holy mountain, also called a hill,
is located in the southern state of Tamil Nadu and is said to be part
of the oldest mountain range in the world. The commanding
Arunachaleswara Temple at its base is dedicated to Shiva and his
wife Parvati (Shakti), and was built in the ninth century AD.
Although I was from a Western background with Catholic roots, I
felt drawn to the Mountain, and the divine energy of Shiva would

transform my life. This would be the true beginning of the journey into the Heart.

My time in India would become interwoven with the dance of Shiva through its many forms and manifestations. I believed I was open before this trip, however, this journey would expose aspects of myself I was still protecting. Moving beyond my limited understanding of the heart, past the seductions of bliss, spaciousness, and unity experiences would become my challenge. The holy mountain Arunachala, along with the direct feedback from David, my teacher, would push me to go even deeper.

The Arrival

With an array of welcoming and sensory overload, India greeted me. Fellow travelers, most of them Indian, hurried past me or pushed me from behind. I found that my American manners of waiting my turn left me standing, while others rushed past. Tightly huddled together, several hundred of us waited for our luggage to come off the airport's conveyer belt. Predictably, next we would be lining up at the money exchange booths. Fortunately, I recalled my friend Dai's advice: first get your money exchanged, then wait for your bags. Sure enough, it worked like a charm. When I returned to the luggage area, the bags were starting to arrive. I needed to overcome my hesitance when I spotted mine. A flurry of jostling for prime position was now in play, as people hovered around with carts and sturdy postures. With a deep breath and few assertive steps, I kindly pushed my way through the crowd, retrieved my backpack, and headed for the exit.

Leaving the brightly lit Chennai Airport in the dark of the night, I walked out into the colorful, busy crowd. With a feeling of relief and gratitude, I spotted a sign "Cathy" and the smiling face of the Indian man holding it. Loading into the taxi, I quickly noticed there were no seat belts for the four-hour journey to Tiruvannamalai still ahead. I felt immediately put at ease when I noticed that the driver had placed an altar on the dashboard, including a picture of Ramana smiling.

The Indian street life and driving were noticeably wild compared to life in America. Everyone seemed to drive fast, confidently dodging any obstacle whether it was a person, cow, dog, or other vehicle at the last possible moment. Varying horn blasts communicated shrilly and often, as vehicles of all sizes maneuvered the roads. I found myself mesmerized by what seemed an overload for my senses: the taxi dodging in and out of traffic, exhaust smells, trash, small fires on the side of the roads, cows and dogs roaming, ox carts, men holding hands, women in their beautiful saris, and the many chai stands blaring loud Indian music. Despite all the motion and seeming chaos, there appeared to be a mysterious order. Only rarely did I observe streetlights, or lines in the road; yet, there seemed to be few accidents. The wandering *sadhus* wearing orange, along with the ancient trees that bordered many roads, seemed like surreal guardians. Their presence seemed to be whispering that a mystical journey had begun.

The further we drove from Chennai, with a population of 7.5 million, the roads became narrow and the landscape rural. Tiruvannamalai is 120 miles southwest of Chennai, and has a population of around 130,000. However, the population can swell to over a million during special full moon and other holy Hindu celebrations. I would be staying in a small village about two miles away, near Ramana Maharshi's ashram. When I spotted towering lights in the night landscape, I knew we were close. It was my first glimpse of the Arunachaleswara Temple, one of the largest in India.

Finally arriving at the guesthouse at two in the morning, I found I could not sleep. I organized my simple room, and wrote in my journal before managing to doze a bit. I awoke when it was still dark before five o'clock in the morning, with a strong urge to go walking. I was apprehensive about venturing out in the dark, but I went anyway. There were people tending their cows, which were tied to the side of the road. I asked for directions to the ashram, knowing the Mountain could be seen from there. Nobody seemed to understand my questions, so I continued walking and ended up at a little chai stand. A devout-looking Hindu man appeared and pulled out a chair for me, then disappeared. As I was about to sit down, I turned around and saw my friend, Dai from the Power of Now Group at Unity looking at me. He had been traveling around India for a few months, and we had been in touch by e-mail. However, we had made no plans to meet that morning. We shared a loving and knowing embrace, smiling at the seeming coincidental meeting.

Dai told me that he had connected with David's *sangha* and we'd be attending the same retreat. He invited me to go on an early walk to the inner path of the Mountain. As we waited for others Dai was meeting, my friend gently nudged me so I could get my first view of Arunachala. When it appeared amid the breaking dawn, I became overwhelmed with emotion: flowing tears, a pounding heart, and a heart full of loving expansiveness nearly caused me to lose my balance. Strangely, an understanding came to me. The Mountain had been calling me to come to India. At that moment, despite the sunrise, a shooting star soared over Arunachala. (The shooting star was especially significant, because the night of Ramana's death in 1950, a meteor passed over Arunachala and was seen in different parts of India. Before his death from cancer, he'd told his grieving devotees that he wasn't going anywhere. The shooting star provided comfort that his words were true. The star arched over the top of the Mountain and vanished.) Dai and I looked at each other acknowledging that we had both seen an omen. We later revealed that we both believed it was a welcome from our beloved Ramana. I knew in my heart, I was home.

The Mother Stone

We left the chai stand, walking along the main road until we reached an opening in the fence that took us to the inner path. Arunachala was illuminated by the sun's glow. I could sense the energy of the Mountain, understanding why it is described as the Mountain of Light and Shiva's Aura. The narrow trail meandered through tall, dry grass until we reached an incline of flat rock that took us to the base of the hill. We continued onto several sacred areas on the Mountain, including an altar where ashes were spread of the spiritual teacher, Papaji, as well as Papaji's Cave. We also visited the Mother Stone, a large cradle of smooth pink, brown, and clear crystallized rock. We took turns lying in it, feeling its nurturing presence. I sent out blessings of love, first to the many people I knew and cared about, including my friends, coworkers, and relatives. The blessings then extended to my guru, those who suffer, those not able to make this sacred journey, and even myself. I laid in the stone cradle feeling its coolness and felt filled with divine Love.

I wrote about the first glimpse of Arunachala and that first day on the Mountain: "I am reminded of a meditation before making plans for this trip. I ended the meditation thinking if I ever glimpse the divine Mountain, I will cry a thousand tears of devotion. It wasn't a thousand tears that I shed, but my first sighting was certainly powerful. Today I am filled with such a peaceful, radiating energy. I feel at home here, as though I could spend the rest of my life here by the Mountain. Thank goodness, the Mountain is within me as the Self. The power of Arunachala is mysteriously beyond all understanding and words."

The Initiation

On the second day I received another sign that I was in the right place. I was wide awake at two o'clock in the morning, still not adjusted to the time change. I got dressed sensing it was time to climb the Mountain. I walked to the main road at 4:30 a.m. It was still dark with the night's mist lingering. Since I did not know where the trail was located, I tried to ask directions from *sadhus* who were wandering in the street. Again, nobody seemed to understand my question. Several Hindus were making their eight-mile pilgrimage around the Mountain, a sacred practice in the region. A devout Hindu woman, perhaps around sixty-five, stopped after overhearing me asking for directions. Speaking no English, she invited me to walk around Arunachala with her. I instinctively said yes. At first I followed her, but soon we were walking side by side. We walked together more than four hours as she visited each of the Hindu temples and shrines along the way.

Westerners are often not welcome into the inner sanctums of Hindu temples, however, as her special guest I was made to feel welcome. In fact, I felt as though I was her adopted granddaughter. With great devotion and care, she adorned my hair with flowers and painted my forehead with special colored ash. She even bought me a cup of chai, and refused to accept my money. Sometimes she would guide us off the road, often to visit a temple I would have never found on my own. This included an old neighborhood temple. We waited quietly outside until it opened, as she shared some nuts she had brought with her for the journey. Then the sleepy neighborhood came to life with the loud ringing of the temple bell. My Hindu grandmother motioned for me to take off my shoes, so we could quickly enter the temple together.

The bell ringer continued to pull the long cord attached to the bell high in the ceiling. His body would repeatedly rise in the air from the weight of the gigantic bell and momentum of its movement. In the darkness and sacred presence we walked past several statues of deities and small fire offerings. The bell continued ringing, clearing my mind of everything except the echo of the last sound, as it was replaced with the next intoxicating deep chime of the bell. A chill crept over my body. Spontaneously, my head started moving side to side and my eyes closed. The sound of the bell became everything as my body and soul seemed to reverberate back into the sound. We sat together in the temple courtyard until the bell stopped. I was overcome with rapture as I arose from the *samadhi* that overtook me.

As we ventured along, within another inner shrine at a smaller temple dedicated to Shiva, the temple priest offered us blessed milk. I felt the sacredness of the temple, grateful that I was allowed to take part in the ceremony. As I drank the consecrated milk, I was again overcome with emotion and chills. Tears of devotion for the Mountain flowed, as I mysteriously felt the energy of Shiva awakening within me. It was as though I had been initiated and welcomed into the Hindu faith. There was no logical explanation for such a powerful emotional reaction; I again felt like I was finally home, as if I had been there before. Everything took on a dreamlike quality. All boundaries seemed to fade. I ambled back to the guesthouse feeling alive and free.

Turned Inside Out

My perception of the Heart Cave, the divine or spiritual center of the heart (my living meditation at the Mountain), seemed to be deepening. On the third day I somehow felt as if I was being turned inside out. I wrote the following in my journal: "Arunachala is the Self. Describing this is difficult but I feel enormously expansive. It is as though everything is flooding in. I am now experiencing the space of the heart beyond the previous physical location that contained it. This shows me that my previous experiences of expansiveness and heart openings have been limited. The lens of awareness suddenly has turned outward beyond the body-mind experience and is inclusive of everything. There is a feeling of welcoming and a knowing that the play of the Divine is at work." It seemed that it was time to simply trust and be guided. I knew Arunachala to be the ultimate symbol of the Heart Cave. It mysteriously includes all, both the manifested and unmanifested. That was the best my mind could do to understand what was happening.

Footsteps of Ramana

On the fourth day I walked from the guesthouse to Sri Ramanasramam, Ramana's ashram, through the back gate and onto a trail that led up the Mountain. I was surprised to note the number of Western spiritual tourists also walking the trail. I made a short visit to Ramana's upper cave, Skandashram, where Ramana lived with his mother between 1916 and 1922. He then moved into the Sri Ramanasramam, which was built after his mother's death. I veered downhill to Ramana's lower cave, Virupaksha, where he lived from 1899 through 1916. Both caves are modernized with white, plaster walls. The lower cave, my favorite, houses several photos of Ramana lining the walls of the outside chamber. I spent the next two hours meditating in the dark and generally quiet, inner chamber.

When I was leaving Ramana's lower cave, I vividly experienced the present moment. I noticed how the activities of my body-mind continued without my effort. Each footstep was for Ramana. My body seemed to be walking his beloved Mountain for him. The simple act of each step, followed by another, or how long I stood on the rocks, or what scenes would draw my attention, demonstrated how the actions of my body-mind simply happen. Who was it that was actually walking? The six hours on the Mountain had a timeless quality, as though a natural rhythm or state of just being had taken over. As I returned to the guesthouse everything I observed was so vivid, all was being experienced as the present moment. It was all Awareness.

Conflict and the Happy Mind

On the fifth day I was surprised to experience a sense of boredom. The quieter my mind, the more evident this feeling of boredom was becoming. After meditating on the roof overlooking a spectacular view of Arunachala I took a short break in my room. When I returned, I noticed my favorite red chair had disappeared. Despite the reality that the chair actually belonged to the guesthouse, my mind was quick to grasp onto something to fret over. I observed and challenged myself over my attachment of needing this specific chair, watching how quickly my mind created a story about who may have taken it and why.

I watched as my mind contemplated what chair I should use instead, as it schemed and weighed potential strategies on how to get my chair back. With my mind now occupied with this problem to resolve, I noticed how my boredom vanished. I reflected on the uncountable times I was content to follow my mind's stories rather than to rest in the experience of quiet and solitude. What a mystery. It seemed I had discovered an important aspect of human conditioning. I laughed at myself; the red chair was so symbolic of our human drama of grasping and aversion. By keeping busy with our petty concerns, we inadvertently avoid experiencing the unknown, the great Mystery, which can only be tasted when we grow quiet.

Purging

After conquering any feelings of boredom, my time in India was about to heat up. The fire of Shiva would be my guide as I faced the unexpected challenge to expose and purge any barriers that protected my heart. Purging was a new concept for me, and a term David used to describe the repression and release of emotional blocks. He taught us that feelings must be experienced through and through in order to be fully observed and let go. If they are not, emotional blocks can express themselves in a variety of physical symptoms. Because other students had often reported purging, I started to believe I was missing something, and my lack of purging meant I was not progressing like other *sangha* members. Yet, my ego would chime in, assuring me that I must be advanced spiritually. I believed I had resolved my childhood traumas and negative life experiences. I concluded that I must already be free and had no need for purging. Though, for a mind like mine that likes to wrestle with problems, I would soon have one.

Messages from the Mountain

After almost a week of being in India, my mind seemed to be settling down nicely. My meditations were spacious and my awareness felt expansive. My thoughts were not dominating my moment-to-moment experiences. During the day's *satsang*, David's monologue revealed specific teachings to several *sangha* members. David called these Messages from the Mountain. He told certain members where they were blocked, and specifically what they needed to do to become free. At other times, he'd recognize someone's progress and validate the choice of an adopted spiritual name. I observed my internal reactions and how I anticipated his words.

I waited for my own progress report from David and message from the Mountain. I imagined any message would be quite positive based on all my spiritual and blissful experiences. No individual message ever came my way. Instead, I was forced to observe my conditioned need for approval. I wrote the following, "If I am free, why do I continue to need approval from my teachers? What does it matter if David, or the Mountain have words for me or not? Maybe the point of all this is to simply witness this tendency arising within me. I do not know."

Life Themes

Coming across a little store on one of my walks to the outskirts of the village, I realized that my Hindu grandmother owned it. Her simple, open-air storefront was nestled between pillars next to a vacant temple. We chatted and I met several of her family members. However, the next morning the negative consequence of drinking homemade lemon soda was apparent. Likely the soda was watered down with tap water, which is one of the leading causes of the dreaded Delhi Belly. I decided to stay in my room to allow the illness to pass, using the time to listen to a talk by Adyashanti[14] on my iPod. I hoped I could make the best of the situation by using the illness as an opportunity to purge, even if it was not officially purging by David's definition.

I created a spiritual practice, becoming mindful of any physical and emotional reactions, especially being open to any insights into my egoic conditioning, (such as self-centered desires, defensiveness, and insecurity). Focusing attention, then breathing into the sensations of any uncomfortable feeling, my practice was to stay open to what I was experiencing no matter what it was.

Adyashanti's talk coincidentally described how a person's conditioning can also be referred to as life themes. I thought of one of mine from the past: "The world and people are not safe and cannot be trusted." Since this didn't seem relevant any longer, I looked at another theme related to my spiritual path, specifically my strong need for approval. This could be seen clearly when I was around David, and to a lesser extent with Joel. I meditated, then wrote the following in my journal: "I spent time with being present with all my perceived imperfections. I felt Arunachala in the core of my being, the heart. I allowed the warmth of healing and the energy of Shiva's fire to burn away feelings of resistance, struggle, and desire."

In the afternoon I attended *satsang*. I talked about how I was using my illness as an opportunity to purge. David acknowledged that I had not done any purging, however, this was not something for me to focus on. He said, "Everything is taking care of itself," adding I should see everything happening around me as a reflection of the inside. I talked to David privately, explaining that I was confused about the concept of purging. I stressed that I wanted to be completely honest with myself. I invited David to share any insights regarding areas of growth I was not seeing. David assured me he would, saying everyone's path is unique.

An Island in Silence

The next day, David gave me feedback I was not expecting. He first confirmed that I was now purging since my illness had lasted a few days. However, he advised that I do the opposite of his usual advice. It was time to let my mind reveal what needed to surface, since spaciousness comes too easily for me. He added, "I have heard you talk about the Heart Cave, but I have never felt it from you." (Ouch.) David continued, "While in all appearances you have obtained freedom, the spaciousness you feel is simply the mask of freedom."

I was instructed to go where it feels uncomfortable, and not to retreat into spacious awareness. This way I could fully be with any arising feelings. "You are not here to be comfortable." I wasn't to understand intellectually what to do by creating a certain practice. Instead, I was to do nothing but exist in the void of unknowing. He said there were still walls of separation in my relationships, and it was time to expose my vulnerabilities. Only then could I love and accept myself fully, including the flawed aspects of myself. If I could hold love for my inner wounded child the walls would start to dissolve.

I felt a crack in my heart, as though a wound had been opened. As this was happening, the witnessing quality within was still engaged, as though what was coming forth had nothing to do with me, and was a wave of emotion just passing through. I wondered at the usefulness of bringing out these painful childhood memories, and allowing my mind to have a heyday with them. I understood that it made sense to bring forth repressed traumas in therapy sessions, yet to do it here in India was not what I had signed up for. Focusing on phenomena arising (emotions, thoughts, and sensations) rather than the spacious gaps from where it all comes from (the unchanging space within) seemed like the opposite of Joel's instruction. David then shook me out of my thinking, saying intensely, "There is no room for an island in silence!" and that it was time for me to address relationships fully. I concluded this interaction in my journal: "So here I am in India in this sacred space being encouraged to cry a thousand tears at Arunachala's feet. The wisdom offered is to be fully honest and just feel through and through."

Seven

Going Through and Through

*God, who is immanent, in his grace takes pity on the loving
devotee and manifests himself according to the devotee's
development.... the guru, who is God incarnate works from
within, helps the man to see the error of his ways and guides
him on the right path until he realizes the Self within.*[15]
~Bhagavan Sri Ramana Maharshi

Go Even Deeper

Despite David's advice catching me off guard, I was
determined to adhere to his feedback and see where it led. To
start, it felt important to shake loose my attachment to my previous
level of spiritual obtainment. I sent off an email to several spiritual
friends in an attempt to expose my spiritual pride and be vulnerable.
It was time to let everyone know the spaciousness I so easily found
has been, as David described, a mask of freedom. I then returned to
the Mountain.

Taking David's feedback to heart, I spent four hours on the Mountain, primarily in Ramana's lower cave. I focused on experiencing my love for Ramana, feeling this love in the heart center. After focusing on my bodily sensations, and the ego identity of Cathy with all the stories, history, strengths and vulnerabilities, a profound deepening or widening of the heart center took place. There were no boundaries or restrictions to this space. I focused on giving loving attention to my body, where I could physically feel emotions that were constricted. Some childhood memories flashed in my mind of stifling tears and sadness, and needing to appear strong.

I immediately sensed a narrowing of my throat and heart space, along with a growing physical sensation of anxiety. The anxiety seemed to be locked in my stomach and chest so that breathing was difficult. I invited Shiva, the deity of fire, to burn away this resistance, fully breathing in the healing energy that surrounded me. The results were extremely powerful. There was an even greater opening within my heart center, best described as freeing. A physical release had somehow occurred, letting go of an area of constriction that had been guarding my heart. I had not realized it had even existed until it was gone.

Leaving the cave, I felt as though the breakthrough had taken place. I went back to *satsang* knowing I had completed the deep work needed. I shared with the *sangha* my experience in Ramana's lower cave, and the deep healing I felt for myself (the child-within). Excitedly, I described the larger space opening within my heart, whispering there were no boundaries to this great love. I knew I must have been beaming. I was ready for David's acknowledgment. It did not come.

David had been listening quietly then firmly gave an unexpected response, "You are still going where it is comfortable. You are still escaping into spaciousness." David advised me to go deeper into the woundedness and to feel that fully. It seemed that he was telling me that I had only tapped into it, but had not fully felt what needed to be experienced, and certainly had not released it. So again the advice was to go even deeper.

Turning up the Heat

Each student needs something different from his or her spiritual teacher, although the student often doesn't understand this. For me, my mind would have liked the relationship with David to be more gratifying to my ego. The spaciousness I had believed was my landmark for freedom was now being discouraged and even confronted. My own knowing and security with my relationship with the Divine was being tested. To trust myself versus trusting David as my teacher was especially on the line. It seemed that David, or the fire of Shiva, was turning up the heat by triggering emotional reactions within me so that I would fully feel or break down. In hindsight, without this heat I would have been content to follow the bliss of my experiences, and live with my still limited understanding of the Heart.

Retracing the Pain

Throughout the night, there were a series of dreams, rambling thoughts, and images from my childhood. There was no sense of emotion or attachment, instead I just witnessed them as if the images were a movie. I awoke early, walked to the inner path, then spent the next seven hours on the Mountain, returning to the Mother Stone where my journey had started. I then was drawn to a large rounded cliff above Papaji's Cave where I laid down in a shallow cave. I would later learn this was Ramana's cliff.[16] I placed seven small stones that were lying nearby on each of my chakra points, then allowed my mind to guide me through images and physical sensations of my past. Before long, I was viewing and remembering many experiences, progressing year by year from my earliest childhood memory to adulthood. Some were joyous, while others were of betrayal, hurt, and rejection. I especially tried to focus on the painful memories.

Yet, I still found myself not losing the spaciousness. I intensely directed attention to the physical sensations of anxiety, anger, and anguish, attempting to avoid where it felt comfortable. Again, there was the return to spaciousness, the center of awareness that remained unchanging. I reminded myself of David's advice to feel things through and through, and continued. Energy freely moved through me without any resistance or clinging. I felt a profound sense of openness to all aspects of life, those considered to be good and bad.

Afterwards, I sat in Papaji's Cave, and mentally invited everyone into the cave I ever felt any resistance, hurt, or anger toward. Before long, the large cave was completely filled. I used the in-breath to bring the energy of any and all feelings into my heart center, feeling them deeply. I visualized that I was holding the child-within with acceptance and love to complete this cycle of healing. After leaving the Mountain I continued to feel an incredible love and spaciousness. My journal concluded, "Each day in India has led to my heart opening beyond what I thought was even possible. I end my day feeling such appreciation to the uncountable people who have touched my life, as even the negative experiences have made my life richer. I wouldn't change anything."

Shiva Shakti

Some *sangha* members talked about sitting with Shiva Shakti, an Amma, or mother of graceful compassion who gives two free *darshans* daily.[17] Her small ashram is a simple open-air room with beautiful marble floors and is located in the village. Shiva Shakti doesn't teach in the traditional sense. Instead, her soft, yet penetrating gaze is said to give powerful transmissions of love. Large crowds come to simply sit in her presence. After my first encounter with Shiva Shakti, I too would return to sit with her at least daily, either late morning or early evening following *satsang* with David. My journal described this first encounter, "I hardly made any eye contact, nor was I even seated in the front row. However, the *darshan* she provided put me into a *samadhi* state several times. I would come out of it and catch her gaze, just to be returned to *samadhi* with one glance from her. I slowly walked back to my room, still immersed in a state of meditative bliss."

Column of Light

The next night was dream-filled and I was walking through many inner temples. Each one was dark, but vibrant with a sacred energy. Each time I'd awake, I would return to the same dream.

Events of the morning were typical of being near the sacred Mountain and not knowing what the day will bring. While sipping chai at a nearby stand, I met a man named Robin from Switzerland. He invited me to visit the Arunachaleswara Temple in Tiruvannamalai, a few miles away. The temple and its grounds are immense. It can easily be seen and heard when walking on Arunachala.

Robin and I flagged down an auto rickshaw to take us to the temple. For a modest donation, a resident swami took us in and became our personal guide. The swami painted our foreheads in traditional Hindu fashion with red, white, and black ash and included us in a blessing ceremony. We were led deeper and deeper into the temple, passing several small fire offerings until we approached the innermost shrine room. It became profoundly quiet. My body was lulled deeper through the winding path into the most inner sanctum. Several Hindu worshipers had gathered around a large, black sacred *lingam*, their object of devotion. A *lingam* or Shiva *Linga* is a phallic-shaped statue said to represent the creative powers of the Universe. We joined the others in the mysterious darkness within the temple's belly. Suddenly, it became light with a vibrant energy. I looked for the source of light but I could not identify anything to account for the brightness. It was like my dream.

Later, I returned to sit among Shiva Shakti's devotees. I had the same experience as my first encounter, yet there was also some type of movement within me. Mysteriously, it was as though Shiva Shakti was working on my heart. Somehow she was penetrating it, opening it up even further with her gaze. My heart ached to the point it felt difficult to breathe. I had the odd sensation of my heart being stretched and pulled from within and without. Nevertheless, I still would return for more.

Later that evening, I returned to the Ramanasramam. I spent some time meditating in Ramana's Old Hall, feeling the presence of my heart. Afterwards, I went to the Mother Shrine and walked the loop to visit all the sacred statues, especially drawn to the statue of the Dancing Shiva and the fire offerings. Feeling a healing and loving energy, I visualized a column of light radiating from the Shiva statue filling my heart, then radiating out for the benefit of all.

The Mountain Violator

With my heart full, I returned for *satsang* the next day. David's energy was intense. It felt serious and a bit intimating. I had never seen him like this. To my surprise, his monologue soon included, "Cathy and her mind's activity has created a violation of the Mountain." (Yikes!) He said that all of my purging was interfering with the silence. He instructed us that this was a precious time to be with the Mountain, and all my socializing and outward activities were distracting away from the Truth.

David then looked at me firmly saying, "I never told you not to meditate, just for you not to do anything." After a period of silence he asked me kindly, "How are you?" When I responded "actually, really good" and briefly mentioned the past few days had been cathartic, David immediately switched from his inviting demeanor to being forceful again, this time directing me resolutely to the Now. He said that nothing else existed except this present moment. David then ended *satsang* early, explaining that this was the first real *satsang* of the trip.

Incredibly confused, I went directly to the Ramanasramam to Ramana's Old Hall to meditate near his couch, which holds a life-size painting of him. I looked into his all-knowing, compassionate eyes. I again worked at holding attention to where it felt uncomfortable and avoided the escape into spaciousness. I recalled David's pointed comments so I could fully experience the sting and bodily sensations of being the bad girl, "The Mountain Violator," being scolded by the father, the beloved teacher, being humiliated in front of the *sangha*, being the trouble maker, the unwanted one, the rejected one, etc. Whatever my mind could conjure and throw at me to make me feel lousy about myself, it was fully welcomed. I allowed any feelings associated with these terms to be present. Again, as all sensations were accepted into my heart they would naturally return to spaciousness.

I continued to allow the waves of physical or emotional discomfort to grow, and I to be with them fully. Once more, they would naturally return to the fullness of the heart. I continued to go where it felt uncomfortable and pushed myself to delve deeper into feelings of rejection, imagining even my friend Dai rejecting me, and disappointed in me. I breathed in the physical sensations of each feeling, experiencing the discomfort fully. Again, it was the beautiful returning into the heart. I wrote in my journal, "Labeling physical sensations as positive or negative is what distracts us away from the natural flow of love. Love is always returning to itself. David is right. It is in feeling things through and through that we become free."

The next day, I returned to Ramana's lower cave where I sat for about two hours before making my way back to *satsang*. My day on the Mountain was a time of being present to whatever I was experiencing. I repeatedly magnified thoughts about being the Mountain Violator to stimulate discomfort, then I would follow the discomfort to its full expression and to its natural dissolving. I continued to remain mindful and detached, yet receptive of all physical sensations arising. They were seen as simply sensations, without the mind labeling the emotional or physical reactions. Increasingly I was becoming comfortable with simply allowing what was arising without resisting or clinging to any experience, sensation, or emotion.

Back at *satsang*, a *sangha* member bravely asked David if one could really violate the Mountain. David responded that he had simply tapped into some forceful energy after spending the day in Papaji's Cave, then answered that nobody could really violate the Mountain. I revealed how I used the feedback as a practice to go into the body and fully feel what it felt like to be the "Mountain Violator." David looked at me silently for a long time then said that while I was the catalyst for his words, it triggered a reaction in everyone. He commented that since I had stayed calm and unmoving throughout, it proved that a part of me was deeply and profoundly free.

In retrospect, I can't help but wonder if David somehow stumbled onto an energy trace left from my emotional work in Papaji's Cave. If that was indeed the case, it sure is funny how life goes around!

Humility and Surrender

David talked about the ego and how the clearest sign that the ego is becoming exposed is the feeling humiliation. If one says I am ready to surrender my ego, this is again a play of the ego. The only thing to trust is the feeling of the heart, that core of our being which is the True Self, the 'I.' If one simply rests and allows this space of the heart to deepen, we can trust that our speech and actions are coming from this place. Otherwise, all is the ego, again reasserting itself.

After *satsang* I went to *darshan* with Shiva Shakti. This time I intended to just be myself with all my human imperfections. I felt her presence as she gazed at me so compassionately. I knew I was fully okay the way I am. It is the mind that creates talk of enlightenment versus ignorance. I thought how none of that even matters. It is just the words formed by our minds and the seeking of the insatiable ego. All that matters is the heart and the energy of this great Mountain. After *darshan,* I felt at peace and that my life was being perfectly guided.

Eight

Meeting Love

There is a love akin to a current in that it flows through all of us. It is this Mountain beyond its form. No love is greater. It belongs to no one yet everyone.

A few days later, I awoke aware that my attention was already resting in the heart space. This awareness must have occurred throughout the night, however, since I didn't recall any dreams. I started my day by attending *darshan* with Shiva Shakti. My heart felt expansive and healed of any blockages. Before long, however, it felt as though her gaze was sawing deep into the core of my being, making the space of my heart even deeper. The energy felt like an intense vibration so that it was difficult to breathe, then followed by a release as though another barrier or shield around my heart was lifted. Each breath felt like a renewal of freedom, as a feeling of love and serenity seemed to fill me.

The Current of Love

After sitting with Shiva Shakti, I went to the Ramanasramam. I spent time in front of the Dancing Shiva statue, praying before moving on to the Old Hall. Near Ramana's couch my heart felt expansive without boundaries. I recognized a vibrant flowing energy as Love, but it had nothing to do with me, nor was it coming from me. It was like a current running through me from the Mountain, this same current on which Ramana, David and others draw. I describe this experience further in my journal: "This current is endless, timeless, has no possession and is owned by no one. It is the purest and truest of any love, of all love. In it, everything arises. It is Consciousness itself. This awareness overwhelmed me bringing tears to my eyes. The birds singing outside perfectly arose out of this space. Not one thing experienced could be differentiated from this Love."

I slowly returned to my room, allowing the awareness and sensations within the heart to be fully experienced. I continued to meditate until it was time for *satsang*. David's monologue coincidentally was about the truest of all loves, the love that I knew

I had experienced. He said that some in the room had tasted this love and explained that if it seems like something you have experienced before, it is not it. Eventually, I described my experience, yet did not use many words. Feeling much gratitude, I described it as the current that connects everyone. It was then David said he could feel my heart.

Lessons from the Flower Sadhu

The next morning I returned to the inner path, and walked the eight-mile loop around the Mountain. I had planned to spend the day in Ramana's caves, however it was as if my legs wanted to keep walking the main road. Not wanting to get lost, I was sure I would turn around. To my surprise, I found the inner path with ease, going past the trail to Papaji's Cave. The path was, at times, quite isolated with only the sounds of nature. This was in contrast to other areas on the Mountain where the sounds of traffic, or the temples could be heard. I saw few people, and simply let myself be guided. Eventually, I returned to the main road in Tiruvannamalai when the thorny bushes made it too difficult to find a trail. I walked on to the outskirts of the city, then with the help from some local people, found another trail that led up the Mountain to Ramana's caves.

On the way to Ramana's lower cave I found a deep red crystallized heart-shaped Arunachala stone. I had collected a few rocks to take home, but this one was the prize. After meditating in the cave and starting to make my way back, I met a friendly and joyous *sadhu*. I nicknamed him the Flower Sadhu. He decorates all kinds of rocks and shrines with colorful flowers. It is his daily practice, and places where he has visited are easily recognized. As I was passing by I could see him sitting in his little grass hut. We exchanged polite gazes; I instinctively bowed to him. At that, the Flower Sadhu hurried out with a big smile holding a few bright red flowers. I thanked him and returned to leave, then stopped to offer him the heart-shaped stone, although I had planned to save it for myself.

He spoke no English, so I did not understand his words, except for the name Shiva. He gestured that Shiva was like the wind and the stone should be returned to the Mountain. His teaching was clear and powerful. I offered the stone to his flower-adorned boulder then returned to the trail with the flowers gently cupped in my hands. The Flower Sadhu reminded me I had everything within me and did not need anything external to make me happy. I then walked past the Wandering Swami who sits and greets people coming up the Mountain. Silently, I offered the red flowers by placing them on a nearby stone, then with a full heart walked away empty handed.

Another Dark Night

My journal described a change in my mental state only a few days later: "The ego (or, more correctly, the mind) is bored with it all. Ready to go home. Ready to leave this spiritual paradise. I am ready to leave this holiest of Mountains. Has completion happened or is this just another delusion? The ego does not get the pats on the head. There is no approval from the master, no keen wisdom, and no bright insights. There are no experiences worth sharing. There is no escaping the Divine Truth, that which stands alone."

During *satsang,* I nearly mentioned how I felt both dead and alive at the same time. However, trying to describe what was going on with me was too difficult. Many in the group were on the verge of awakening, or were free as David says. A feeling of dullness had taken over. I was left to question whether my recent heightened spiritual experiences and insights had only added to my delusion. Yet, there was still the Self utterly unchanged through all of these thoughts and emotions. My journal describes my confusion further: "There is no food for the ego here. Yet, there is no giving up, nowhere to go and nowhere to escape. My mind is spinning. I have nothing to hold onto. I feel empty, almost like I would love to just vomit in order to rid myself of this lie, this fake identity that is not the Self. Shiva, help me. There is nothing more I can do. My heart is now open, yet my mind is full of doubt. My spirit feels empty without a spark. I am dying. It is the burn. *Om Arunachala Shiva.*"

The disheartened state continued, and only deepened throughout the day. I finally felt hopeless enough to meet privately with David. He told me it was a good sign I was going through this, advising me to go into the feeling without trying to change it. He believed it was part of the cracking open only possible when one is able to reach a deeper level of self-exploration. David described it as the dark side wanting to be exposed and accepted. I reminded him of someone who is not truly free because she has been unwilling to complete the deep work. While this person is helping people, she has not faced the dark side, so cannot be fully free.

Later I wrote, "I am watching my mind. At times my ego even wants to own how badly I feel, trying to make a mind drama out of it. So far, I am not getting lost in my mind's attempt to seduce me back into ignorance. The hopeless feeling has now continued into the night. It has now lessened some, leaving a feeling of defeat. I surrender, there is nothing I can do. What will be will be."

Hollow Shell

The next morning I awoke before dawn. Besides it being too hot to sleep, I felt physically ill. I sat on my bed and tried unsuccessfully to meditate, then drifted in and out of sleep as I tried to relax. All sorts of stories and visions started rushing into my mind. Oddly, these stories were not about me, nor about anyone I knew. I felt empty of myself. It was as though I was merely a witness, no longer participating in form. I then had an unusual and vivid dream that a ghost inhabited my body following a tragic, fiery accident. Death was everywhere as I watched how others were leaving their bodies. The jolt of a ghost entering my body was so sudden it made me start coughing, then vomiting. Some people tried to help me by patting my back. I finally lay on the ground experiencing absolutely no fear as the ghost fully inhabited me. I had become a hollow shell. I surrendered to a pleasant sensation of dizziness as I dissolved into the inner light. I became lucid as I rose to leave the accident scene. I offered prayers to Ramana, Arunachala, and Shiva.

When I awoke a few hours later I felt incredibly refreshed, and somehow purified. Mysteriously, I knew it was time to climb to the top of the Mountain, something I had not yet attempted. I packed a small backpack and left early from the guesthouse, knowing I was to journey alone in silence.

Secrets from Arunachala

I followed the trail to Ramana's upper cave then started to climb a section of smooth but steep rock. It was slippery and at times difficult to keep my footing. Just as I wondered if maybe this wasn't such a good idea, a few locals yelled at me from below, pointing toward an easier trail. Thankful for the timely guidance that the Universe provided, I hiked to the new trail. Although still steep, this one offered many rocks positioned like stairs. I continued my journey feeling divinely guided.

My seven hours on the Mountain seemed to complete the purification process begun in the night. A timeless and almost magical quality enveloped the whole experience. I spent over three hours on top of Arunachala. All visitors must remove their shoes as a sign of respect, as Shiva is ever present on top of the Mountain. Barefoot, I felt the warmth and stickiness of the sacred black coating, the residual of endless layers of burned ghee, or clarified butter, which coats the red stone beneath. Several young *sadhus* were on the Mountain top, as well as other tourists. To create some privacy, I hiked to a narrow cliff just below the peak and meditated, feeling the presence of my expansive heart.

Somehow on my way down from the Mountain I made a wrong turn, and for a time it seemed like I might be lost. To my surprise, a vacated cave dedicated to Shiva was located along this new path. The cave seemed to be inviting me to linger, so I did for a few more hours. After returning to my room I wrote, "I cannot say what this all means, however I have never felt more alive. I feel love more deeply than I ever have. I feel the divine presence to the core of my being. Today was a union with the Divine Consciousness in its many forms: Shiva as the wind, the Mountain itself, the rocks, hawks, people, lizards, the blue dragonflies circling around the top, and even with myself. I experienced the light of Shiva radiating in my body and am still filled with a loving presence."

Afterwards I attended the final *satsang* with David, since the *sangha* was leaving for the U.S. in the evening. I would be staying on for another five days. I gave sincere thanks to David for his direct teachings and guidance. His feedback brought light to the dark sides of myself and pushed me to a deeper journey. My journal continued, "I am overwhelmed by the grace that has brought me to this sacred Mountain, and the growing Presence I can now feel within my heart."

Even This

My remaining days in India would include visits to Shiva Shakti for *darshan*, spending time in meditation, and being with life as it was presenting itself. As I was walking in the village several scenes caught my attention, such as a struggling ox pulling a heavy cart and a beggar with a badly infected eye. I felt the words creep up inside me, "Even this is God . . . Even this is God." The words were coming from the core of me and would arise when I would witness an emotionally-challenging scene, typically of a person or animal suffering. As I made my way to the Arunachaleswara Temple in the adjoining city, I observed how my tolerance for what I was experiencing had grown significantly since my arrival. Mother India then seemed to test my growing acceptance and tolerance of what I was witnessing.

Near the end of my trip, I became entangled in a large crowd leaving the Arunachaleswara Temple. After spending so much time in quiet and meditation, the scenes of life unfolding around me felt electric like a vibrant pulse of humanity. The street life was a flurry of activity with its colorful array of fruit and flower stands, and all sorts of vendors selling spices and goods. The ripe presence of trash mingled with the enticing smells of incense and food stands. Everything seemed to have its place in this spectacular display. Pedestrians along with daring bicyclist dodged the zip of agile motorcycles and auto-rickshaws that squeezed between the trucks and buses that dominated the road. The roar of traffic, mixed with bellowing horns and the rhythmic sounds of drums and bells coming from the temple added to the zeal of the moment. I found myself perched on a raised median waiting for oncoming traffic to pass so I could cross the busy street.

It was then I noticed something in the road ahead of me. It was a disabled man with missing limbs lying helplessly on the side of the busy road. He had some sort of palsy and appeared greatly paralyzed. His limited movements seemed to grind his mostly bare skin deeper into the hot and gritty pavement. Obviously he was completely dependent on others to care for him. He wore only a loincloth, and had no sunglasses to shield his eyes. His skin looked dark, leathery, and reddened from the sun's glare.

The drums from the temple continued beating. My eyes continued to follow his movements as if he were moving in synch with everything going on around him. There he lay covered in the dirt from the street. Motorized rickshaws, trucks, taxis, and the crowd of pedestrians swerved to avoid him as he lay there moving side to side. I then noticed a large and prominently displayed black begging pot on his chest. He was obviously incapable of placing the pot on himself nor getting in the road by himself. I deduced that his caregiver would place him out in the street to beg and likely was standing nearby to collect any money. I looked directly at him, feeling compassion but did not give money. I then felt the clear message come once more, "And even this . . . even this is God."

The Dance of Shiva

My final days in India included several hours gazing at the Dancing Shiva statue in the Ramanasramam. Seeing the Shiva clothed in leopard-print pants seemed strange at first, yet there was something mysterious about its presence. I noticed the statue when visiting the Mother Shrine at the ashram my first day, and since had been progressively mesmerized by it. I wondered what was this dance about. There were so many arms and different symbols I did not understand. However, in the presence of the figure I was beginning to glimpse the truth of how resistance occurs in daily life, and how the dance of abiding is what sets us free.

I wondered how I could approach and live my life with the spontaneity, grace, and pleasure of this cosmic dancer. Effortlessly, the question was answered immediately as if by a mysterious transmission. *I* was the Shiva statue dancing. *I* was this spontaneity and grace. Shiva was I; I was Shiva. I felt a release of all effort as I realized there was nothing to resist or avoid, and nothing to run from or to run toward. There was only Shiva capering and whirling through all the changes and obstacles of life, and no difference between the movements of abiding and resistance. In the dance of Shiva or play of God, these actions and events in life were seen as part of the whole. It was Shiva twirling through the joyous times, as well as dancing through the times of challenge, pain, and even confusion. In the presence of this figure, I was learning to live life with the willingness and acceptance of the dance.

I knew I had discovered a tool, a coping strategy I could access anywhere and any time. My journal concludes the insight gained: "The more I accept everything into my life, the more I experience everything to be One. However, the more I resist something, anything, the more separate I become from what is happening around me, thus maintaining the illusion of separateness. In Consciousness, there is only One. It is all the dance of Shiva, which is Love. Living fully is the dance."

The Mountain Within

My heart felt brimming as I thought of leaving India the next day. I again spent several hours on the Mountain, which included receiving a powerful blessing from the Flower Sadhu. Looking into his eyes brought tears, since the energy of the Mountain and a stream of love seemed to pour from him. I realized our eyes were both seeing emptiness, yet reflecting everything to each other. I left him feeling an intense expansiveness of a loving heart as I walked down the Mountain trail. This time the Flower Sadhu gave me a large handful of yellow and red flowers. I walked with the bundle of flowers placing a clump of yellow flowers on a stone as an offering to the Mountain. My body walked further down the Mountain then suddenly stopped. It felt as though I could go no further, even though I was not physically tired. Sitting on a large, inviting stone nestled under a shade tree, I closed my eyes while the light breeze caressed and cooled me.

In loving gratitude tears of devotion for Arunachala, Shiva, and Ramana flowed, as if I were an empty vessel being filled by the Mountain's presence. All sense of separation from what was being seen and experienced outside of myself dissolved. Mysteriously, the presence of the Mountain was now within me. I was the Mountain, and the Mountain was I. Spontaneously, I opened my hand that held the remaining flowers and offered them to people who were walking up the Mountain trail. The gesture felt symbolic of how everything is a return to the Mountain, to the Divine. I sat absorbed in being the Mountain. There were no thoughts, no identity, only the silence and energy of union.

A bright-eyed Israeli tourist, a woman I'd met earlier, came down the Mountain trail. She smiled as she handed me a clump of yellow flowers. I immediately recognized the flowers as the same ones I had placed on the rock much further up the trail. A feeling of unity overwhelmed me as it seemed that this gesture was teaching me that the current of love was flowing endlessly downstream from the Mountain. The Mountain was not something separate from me. There was nothing that I could be parted from. My journal completes the story: "The Mountain is the stillness within each of us. The energy just spreads by itself through every kind gesture, every act of love, and when we slow down enough to taste the wind. The message was clear. It was time to bring home the Mountain. My heart in its unlimited capacity for love could contain even this Mountain. Oh, this love."

My last day in India was a blessed one. It began with a final journey into love's endless stream with Shiva Shakti, I felt blessed by her compassionate gaze. At the end of *darshan* her parting nod seemed to tell me I was ready. I was ready to return to the world, to spread this eternal love. My journal continues, "The opening into love is the Self. Oh, this has been such a magical journey, a true journey into the endless depths of the Heart."

PART IV:

Witnessing the Confused Mind

Nine

Half Home

*Freedom is revealed when Consciousness is recognized as
everything, including the perception of being a separate self.
The test for freedom is whether we can recognize
Consciousness even in the perceived struggles that may be
happening.*

Slowing Down

W ithin a few days after returning home from India, I was back
at work. The noise and constant motion of the hospital
setting jarred my nerves. I wondered if I would ever return to my
previous busy pace and productivity. Many coworkers would ask
about my trip to India: "What was the best experience? What was
your favorite thing? Did you get sick? Weren't you afraid?" Some
would wait for an answer, but most were already busy, moving onto
the next activity or task. They reminded me of myself when I had
first arrived to India.

Excited to write about my first adventure-filled day in India, I
arrived at a home-based internet business to send e-mails home. A
man wearing sunglasses was sitting in the courtyard. He appeared
relaxed and was reading a newspaper. To complete the scene a

golden-colored dog slept and several tourists casually sat in lawn chairs under the bamboo roof. I asked the man how long it would be before I could use a computer so I could plan the rest of my day. He looked at me curiously and responded in a slow Australian accent, "Do you have somewhere you need to be?" It dawned on me that I really did not. I gleaned a little insight as I felt the impatience I had brought from my busy life in the States. He then smiled and said, "You look like you are in more of a hurry than I am, why don't you go ahead of me?" Soon I was sending off my e-mails feeling a little guilty for appearing so obviously impatient, but not giving it much more thought. It would take several days until the value of his teaching would fully reveal itself.

Quite in contrast to the wild traffic conditions in India (with its various vehicles competing with the wandering cows), the walking pace in India is actually quite slow. Ramana Maharshi even taught that one should walk like a pregnant woman while on the Mountain. Things are often done slower in India. When someone says the wait for a certain service will not take very long, this could still mean several minutes to hours or even days. People also appear more accepting and relaxed about what is happening around them, even if they suddenly need to dodge an oncoming vehicle. The longer I remained in India, the more I sensed my own patience and tolerance increasing. I was finally starting to slow down and relax on a deeper level than I had ever experienced. My walking pace became slower, and I was not in such a rush to get somewhere.

About a week later I was back waiting for a computer, casually sitting in a plastic chair under the bamboo roof. The same golden dog was there and chose to rest near my feet. Although reading material was available, I was content just to sit, do nothing, and wait. A man, likely an American, hurried into the shaded courtyard; talking fast and asking when a computer would be available. I flashed on the memory of myself that first day. I was considering whether I should ask if he had somewhere he needed to be and offer my spot to him. However, he was too inpatient to wait for my response and left. I recognized myself and how harried I must have looked to that Australian tourist. I reflected on how I have battled impatience much of my life. It seemed that the peace and quiet inside me were counter to my own conditioning.

Now, back in the States, I felt empathy for my coworkers and family members for the times they had to tolerate my heightened anxiety and impatience. It struck me how we are all perfect images for one another if we slow down enough to see it. I felt thankful to that first Australian tourist and the American who so reflected myself back to me.

For some time the pace of India stayed with me. While a slower rhythm was my preference, I discovered I could still work fast when needed. The difference was the inner drive of excitement and adrenalin I used to thrive on was no longer present. Curious, I wondered what was motivating my actions and realized that my self-worth had always been closely tied to being extra efficient and being one of the most productive workers. I recognized the pleasure this brought and how it was mostly ego-driven. A shift was happening within me. Instead of the inner drive for productivity, based on lacking and trying to prove myself, there was a growing trust in the wisdom, or simplicity, of being present.

I sensed how spaciousness permeated all aspects of my life, so tasks were completed but with less effort and less stress. It was paradoxical to logical thinking. I no longer needed to try so hard. A witnessing quality was ever present as life unfolded around me. The more I lived in this space of inner silence, the more I was at peace, even when engaging in the extroverted life of a social worker. Being present was so natural, and things that needed to get done would, without me needing to stress about them. Unfortunately, this increased comfort of simply abiding in the present moment only lasted for about a month.

Lost

Soon I returned to feeling the stress of my job. I struggled to meet the demands of the householder's life, and worried that somehow I had lost the insights that had given me such peace. While I could still observe my feelings and emotions arising so clearly, and was seeing through the eyes of the inner witness, I was feeling increasingly separate.

I wondered if half of me was still in India and if I needed to return to find myself once more. The great openings of connectedness and unity I had experienced had now melted into utter confusion. I felt disconnected from my work environment and from both of the *sanghas* where I was a member. My mind continued to create its own story about the distance between what I had experienced in India, and what reality was like in the United States. I felt lost.

Watching my struggles, Steve encouraged me to attend the weekly group at the Center. I felt reluctant about returning that particular evening, feeling emotionally and spiritually fragile. I did not want to show this vulnerable side of myself. Soon after Joel rang the bell to begin the meditation I remembered David talking about the movement of expansion and contraction. I remembered how any time we feel resistance to something it is the action of contraction. On the other hand, what we welcome, such as the feelings of bliss and love, is the action of expansion. I could again feel these movements within my heart. I immediately realized that this was why I had been suffering. I had experienced many episodes of expansiveness in India. Back in my normal life I now found myself experiencing contraction.

With this recognition it all dissolved immediately. It was as though any feelings of disconnectedness had never existed. I drew a deep breath and released it slowly, knowing nothing had ever changed. I had been listening to the stories of my own mind, which had led me away from resting in the natural essence of who I really am. Something significant released and my heart seemed to crack wide open. Silent tears of gratitude started to flow as my mind cleared and a feeling of release and freedom came about as I simply followed the breath and returned to just being. All was arising out of the Heart of Awareness. Even the chair in front of me I knew to be Consciousness. As the separation between my body and what was around me dissolved, the taste of grace filled my soul like an old friend.

The Student Teacher Dance

I trusted my own spiritual insights again. I knew they were pointing to the Truth. However, my mind still wanted to label my experiences, many of them intense and significantly heart opening. I believed I must have awakened, and that I had learned all I needed from my spiritual teachers, and was ready to journey on alone. On one level this was true, because while a teacher or guide is extremely helpful at different stages of the path, we eventually need to rely on our inner guidance and trust our own insights. Although this seemed appropriate at the time, it was premature.

My recognition of the pervasiveness of Consciousness was still unstable. I was still giving thoughts authority and I was falling into one of the seductive traps my mind would set for me. Wanting to be a good student, and prone to spiritual perfectionism, I yearned for validation from my teachers. I was seeking outside myself, instead of resting in my own knowing. Before long I would again chase my elusive self in circles, trying to find the one truth that would tell me that I was free. However, continually seeking an outside authority to place the invisible stamp on my awakening made the distinction between student and teacher stronger and strengthened the separate self that sought freedom. Before long I was again lost in my thoughts—not enlightened but entranced.

Spiritual Suffering

In April, I attended another five-day retreat at Cloud Mountain. This one was called "Testing the Teachings" given by Joel, and Tom McFarlane who is a long-time member of the Center. We were instructed to verify the truth of our experiences through teachings, choiceless awareness meditations, and even some magic tricks. This would be a challenging retreat for me, as my mind was still trying to process what had occurred in India since returning home.

My journal described my mental state, "In a nutshell I am out of sorts, out of balance, dwelling in my mind more than I care to admit. I do not know what I am doing half the time. There are so many moments and episodes of clarity and connectedness, and then I am crazily over-reactive and confused about what drives my actions. People often ask me about India and my spiritual practice. Currently I feel like such a fake. I was doing fine, and now I feel more confused than ever. So I start this retreat feeling quite deflated and humble."

On the second day of the retreat, I wrote the following: "Despite this being a good retreat as far as teachings and the clarity during meditations, I am allowing my mind to lead me down a dark path. I feel conflicted and wondering if I am totally off track spiritually. My confusion seems to be about David and whether I should fully trust his teachings. I don't know if I am deluding myself or not. If my mind just knew for sure, I could finally relax into my own knowing. I know this is just another trap of the mind I am falling prey to. Why do I continue to do this?"

By the third day I was thinking about leaving the retreat. I had never been tempted to leave a retreat early before, so I knew this was a sign that something was really wrong. The feeling of unease continued. Late in the evening I finally went to talk to Joel. It was no doubt the longest talk we ever had. I talked about David, his teachings, about purging, experiences in India, and of my confusion and recent suffering. I discussed openly my perception of awareness. Joel said he would not call my experience awakening or gnosis (realization). If so, I would be free from all doubts and would not be seeking any confirmation. I agreed with him, yet I could not say that he was right. My journal described this interaction further: "The perception of awareness I have is not a state and has not changed. In the end, Joel said that only I could know for sure. Whatever the label, I cannot accept Joel's words that I am not aware of the Self or Self-realized. This I know to be true. While it would be more settling (for my mind) to have confirmation from my spiritual teachers, it does not change this space. Nothing has changed."

Regarding David, Joel encouraged me to use my intuition and decide who my primary teacher should be, as he acknowledged some clear differences that could be adding to my confusion. In particular, there were big contrasts to his regarding abiding in spaciousness, compared with David's advice. He suggested I choose a primary teacher and stick with one.

An Open Vessel

During a guided meditation, I could see how being present always points to our true nature. Anyone can find his or her true nature; it is here all the time. I could feel this awareness or presence growing within me. At one point, Tom instructed the group to be like an empty vessel. This phrase was especially powerful. It immediately cued me to be more aware during meditations, and an open, receptive presence when not meditating. I could sense already being filled with Consciousness, how there was only spaciousness, and being an open vessel for it all.

The next morning Joel and Tom instructed us to spend the day in solo practice, integrating the teachings. I spent the day being a witness to sound, my focus for studying impermanence, and being an open vessel. I discovered there is nowhere for sound to return to; there is only Awareness. Joel advised us to follow sound from its arising, such as a bird calling, then following the sound with attention to the last note or call. After attentively following sound and paying attention to my own experience, it became clear that silence and sound are the same. Both are the same in Consciousness. It is all revealing and returning.

In the afternoon, I napped and had an odd dream about witnessing my face disintegrating. I was out of my body observing as my eye was caving in, then my nose. I knew this was all a part of impermanence, yet nothing really changes. There was no fear or concern, just a curiosity and willingness to have the process completed. I awoke out of the dream, the disintegration still incomplete.

Lightening up on the Path

I met with Joel again, who advised me to not take the path so seriously. He suggested that I study the Buddha's Four Noble Truths[18] and explore the nature of suffering. The Noble Truths are as follows: Life means suffering; the origin of suffering is attachment;

the cessation of suffering is obtainable; and there is a path to the cessation of suffering. He recommended that I try to determine if I was suffering. I decided to use that as a guide. Again, he repeated that I was the only one who knew with certainty my awareness. He described how there was no self and no doer, that it is Consciousness that leads the dance of life. I wondered how it was possible that the currents of unease occur on the unchanging surface of awareness? And, why did I become so seduced into their story?

The retreat ended the next afternoon. I drove home with three others. Toward the end of the drive I talked about my spiritual crisis and my recent experiences of awareness. One fellow spiritual seeker pointed out that if I were having any doubts, this was a sure sign that I am not awake. I acknowledged this, yet I concluded my journal entry with the following, "Nothing has changed within me regarding this awareness despite the feedback and the episodes of mental unrest. Still, there is witnessing of all arising and a return to the space within that does not change."

Reflecting back on this period, I was still missing the crucial insight of no self, despite my deepening awareness and the witnessing quality that was occurring in my life. I was failing to recognize that all that was arising, even my identification with thoughts, were as much a part of Consciousness as everything else. Spiritually, I still only had one eye open.

Ten

Dropping Ever Deeper

There is but one God, witness of all, hidden in all creation,
absolute, pervading all,
the inner Self of all.[19] *~Bhagavan Sri Ramana Maharshi*

Dropping In

For the next few months following the retreat, I continued to vacillate between trusting myself and doubting my knowledge of the truth. My mind was still busy processing what happened during the trip to India. I questioned whether it was my own ego that didn't want David's guidance, or if I had truly completed the work I was to accomplish with him.

Finally in July it seemed the confusion was lifting, and I was back on track spiritually speaking. I wrote, "For the past week there has been an aching of a full, yet yearning heart. Inquiring into this space brings me further into the Mystery. I am just letting myself fall into it. My mind remembers similar feelings of this energy prior to making plans to go to India. Yet, I do not know what this means or what is being revealed. It just is, and inexplicably I have full trust in it."

I returned to the Center and started attending regularly, discovering a renewed connection to Joel as my primary teacher. A growing humility was also developing that I had more to learn. I was beginning to wonder if the spiritual path ever ended. An unexpected deepening happened at the Center a short time later. Joel led us in a choiceless awareness meditation based on the teachings of the Tao Te Ching. He asked us to generate a thought then watch it completely dissolve into emptiness. He had us practice this three or four times with different thoughts, watching each thought completely dissolve. By following the thoughts in a relaxed manner there was simply empty awareness. Without thoughts being generated, there was no sense of me as "Cathy." I was only this emptiness, nothingness. It was so clear that I was nothing, and all was empty. I knew there to be only Awake Consciousness. The insight flashed that there was no true beginning or ending, and no death. All was still arising and passing away within Consciousness. I knew Consciousness, God, doesn't go anywhere.

I talked to Joel afterwards. I described the opening and dropping in to a deeper level of experience. I knew Consciousness to be boundless, beyond my previous understanding. Joel recommended continued meditation practice and studying the Dzogchen Teachings. I admitted that I had learned that relying on Grace rather than trying to repeat a certain practice often worked better. Joel suggested that I just show up for the practice with an open heart and open mind, and allow the Divine to show me what it will. He said it was also okay if the Divine revealed nothing, then the next time show up completely so the Divine can reveal its dance.

Melting into this Great Mystery

Through the summer this feeling of dropping in or melting deeper into my heart continued. I was experiencing a penetrating and expansive sense of emptiness frequently. Resting in this space of unknowing was comforting and peaceful, but alarming for my mind at the same time. I would have thoughts that nothing would be revealed spiritually by just resting in stillness and doing nothing.

Yet, my heart center ached with openness, stilling my mind and making me outwardly a quieter person.

Working in a busy hospital and engaging in the normal affairs of a householder continued, yet my attention was not being entranced by the busy thoughts of doing and planning. I could still socialize and carry on in my outward life, and in all appearances life was the same. However, the inner witness was fully engaged. I was attuning to the expansiveness of my own heart, sensing the inner stillness growing within me. I was finally relaxing into myself, best described as coming home.

Mountain Calling

By early fall, somehow I knew I would return to India, and made plans to do so. I would be gone for a month and would travel alone. I decided not to join David's group for their annual retreat to Arunachala. They would be arriving the first part of February, and I would be leaving India shortly after. Finally, I had come to terms with my separation from David as my teacher, and believed that I had moved on. Then mysteriously, it seemed it was time to see him again. I decided this must simply be to connect with *sangha* members, since in India it was likely that I would run into a few members around the village and ashram. I planned to drive to Portland alone to attend a half-day intensive, believing I needed to process my next steps. However, to my surprise, Consciousness had other plans. Following a short retreat given by Tom Kurtza in Eugene, I connected with a few of David's *sangha* members who were also attending. We spontaneously planned to attend David's *satsang* together.

We drove to Portland the next morning, and I was feeling a little apprehensive. Not wanting to draw attention to myself, I sat towards the back of the crowded room. David's monologue was about staying committed to the spiritual path, even in times of adversity. He said it is important to understand that the hardships and forms arising outside ourselves are mere projections of our own minds. If there is a self and other, then one is not completely free. Only in true freedom can love be felt through and through without a feeling of separateness. I was attentive during *satsang,* but also took Joel's advice, which was to be an active observer. I couldn't help but acknowledge that this teaching seemed perfect for me, and what I had been going through.

I was going to leave quickly afterwards, feeling that it was likely my last time attending. As I was making a donation and signing the guests' roster, David hollered at me not to leave without saying hello. I stayed to talk to him. His greeting felt genuine and kind. To my surprise, I told him honestly that I did not believe that we had a good connection as a student and teacher, but I sincerely thanked him for pushing me to go deeper. I continued that I knew there was no difference between us in spaciousness, but explained that I felt a distance and separation between us as people. David replied that within him there was only love flowing toward me. He continued that since I had been away he has felt the loss that one would feel toward a child who has died, that he has missed me. He said that in my relationship with the unmanifested and with my connection to Shiva that I am completely free. However, in relationships between people, while much had been healed, in this area I was not completely free.

David said that it was through *our* relationship that opening to limitless love was possible. He spoke of the divine union being like two lovers meeting beyond form. So this is what I was left with. He continued to invite me into union with him, coming together with a full and loving heart, and if I wanted to work on being absolutely free in my relationships, the work needed to be done with him. I wrote the following, "It just seems like such a step back to return to a teacher-student relationship with David. I guess I am at a loss of what I should do."

PART V:

The Journey into the Heart Cave

Eleven

Fire in the Heart

All dwells in the Heart Cave, the Radiant Heart. It is Shiva's
Universe, the sacred Om.

Being Lost without a Plan

O ctober approached. All of my past conditioning had
programmed me well about the necessity of creating a plan
and strategy, of how to conduct myself in life, and even a back-up
plan, but now much seemed to be unknown. I found myself at times
musing on how we do not know what is going to happen anyhow,
even with all our planning and strategic thinking. We can make
plans, take our best guess on how things will turn out, but really we
still do not know for certain. Somehow, the uncertainty of life felt
freeing and I felt more open and trusting.

My journal described this: "I am in the fire of the unknown. At
another point of my life I would have felt too uncomfortable in my
own skin to bear it. Change is coming. I do not know what the
results will be, but I do not see myself living my life as I have been
living it. At work, I feel less social, choosing the quiet over group
lunches. The quiet within is taking over, and I am seeking ways to
create it. Even if it is just taking a breath of awareness, to pause and

witness the momentum of what is going on within and around me, that is becoming enough. My life feels in some ways that it is falling apart, yet, there is a feeling of welcoming whatever is happening."

A Retreat for the Bhakti

Mid-October, I attended a powerful retreat given by Joel at Cloud Mountain, appropriately called, The Fire in the Heart. It was a retreat about the Bhakti path of devotional practices, compared to the Jnana teachings of Vipassana and self-inquiry meditations.

Joel told us that you can choose to be a Jnani searching for Truth, but you cannot choose to be a Bhakta since it comes from Grace. There needs to be an invitation, an inner experience within your heart that then changes your life. Listening to the introduction, I knew I was in the right place. My heart was already aching with devotion and felt emotionally vulnerable. We were to announce what our devotional mantra would be for the duration of the retreat, and then stick with it since the mind gets easily bored and may try to do something else. I said mine would either be, "*Om Namo Shivaya*, or *Hum Shiva*." I also mentioned that I wasn't sure if I could complete a whole retreat with this mantra without feeling emotionally overwhelmed. Joel said matter-of-factly, "Don't think about it, just do it!" (Sound advice.)

In the evening I settled into my room, set up an altar, and taped pictures on the wall. Surprisingly, as I was packing a few things from home, I was drawn to bring pictures of the two *sanghas*. One was a group photo of a retreat with Joel, the other was of David's group with Arunachala in the background. These photos were to remind me that all is Consciousness. That evening I wrote, "While saying my mantra, I looked up at the pictures of the *sanghas*. Suddenly, a blissful surge rushed through me, bringing tears to my eyes. The words, "Form is Emptiness, Emptiness is Form" came like a revelation. I knew this was the reason I was at the retreat, and that this was the lesson David had tried to teach me. It felt as though this was the time to know this fully.

The Four-Heart Meditation

Joel instructed us to begin the retreat. The first step was to study the impermanence of thoughts, then to study impermanence in nature. This helped us slow down our busy thoughts, encouraging greater mindfulness for the meditations to come. We meditated as a group, witnessing thoughts coming and going. I searched to find who creates the thought to begin with, and their origin. Again, the answer revealed the space within that remains the same.

Joel told us the next several days would be spent meditating on the Four Hearts of the Bhakti Path, including the Physical Heart, Emotional Heart, Spiritual Heart, and Radiant Heart. He explained that we were learning the Prayer in the Heart, and how each step would lead us deeper.

Four Heart Meditation (Prayer in the Heart), by Joel Morwood

1. **Physical Heart**. Bring attention to the physical heart space by following the breath. The mantra (or sacred word) is invited to reside in the heart, then slowly repeated.

2. **Emotional Heart**. Continue to repeat the mantra with a feeling of love and longing, allow feelings to surface; then watch them come and go. Allow attention to rest in this space, alertly observing how all emotions are still rooted in love and longing. If this is difficult, get in touch with any sort of self-centered longing until this is recognized.

3. **Spiritual Heart**. This is a space of Consciousness and clarity. Continue to repeat the mantra, allowing all arising phenomena (even spiritual experiences) to come and go in choiceless awareness. Simply feel or sense the Divine's presence in this space of the heart. Effort is then dropped.

4. **Radiant Heart**. Allow the mantra to end on its own, so that there is a dropping into a profound silence or spaciousness. This is the space of non-dual reality, God without form, the true heart center or seat of Consciousness. In the core center there is nothingness. Without thoughts or other phenomena arising, Gnosis (Realization) is possible.

After several rounds of meditation, I could feel the expanse of my heart growing to the point it would ache. When I followed my mantra into the heart space, it dissolved into the silence of the spiritual heart. Following the mantra so deep into the heart space opened into the void, immediately revealing what I only knew as the Heart Cave.

Joel explained that this journey leads us from the spiritual heart to the Radiant Heart. If the mind is truly quiet, and spaciousness is all that we experience, we may enter a state of *samadhi* (complete absorption where all becomes One). The quietness of this Radiant Heart space is what Ramana Maharshi called the Pure Radiant Heart of Consciousness or the 'I.' The Heart is everything and becomes everything. While it is wonderful hanging out in this space, Joel said we could move even deeper through some self-inquiry.

I wrote the following, "Wow. The Heart Cave is not an inward dwelling, a small cave where one can hide from the outside world. All in its splendor is revealed. Everything is turned inside out, similar to what happened in India. This time, it includes all forms, all sounds, everything. All dwells in the Cave of the Heart—This is the Radiant Heart. I am overcome with the bliss of this divine disclosure. It's Shiva's Universe, the sacred Om."

Awakening the Hardened Heart

The teachings continued. The hardened heart is one of the obstacles of the Bhakti Path. This comes from a lifetime of trying to protect ourselves from risk and pain, and leads to feeling restriction or contraction in the heart center. Joel taught us about waking up the heart so it could lead us back to the Source, back to God. Even resistance can be transformed. He talked about reaching further into the heart until it is broken through and through. If one's heart is completely shattered, it will never be broken again. What is called for is a sincere understanding that lasting happiness cannot be found in a person, or worldly things. If one fully understands this, then one will naturally turn further inward, at first to a level of total despair and hopelessness, which will transform into the ultimate surrender of that fairy tale.

An attendee asked Joel an interesting question: "Can someone wake up if the emotional heart is not purified?" Joel answered, "Yes, like Ramana Maharshi. One can suddenly wake up and all is revealed and purified. However, for most, there will be gnostic flashes. Because the emotional heart is not purified, one will soon return to their ego tendencies." I wondered if maybe this is what had been happening to me.

I continued to meditate on my own until it felt my heart had reached a new level of understanding. My journal continued, "My prayers to Ramana and Shiva have been answered. I have been given wondrous glimpses into the divine manifestation of form, which is not separate from myself. I now understand the gift of David's teachings. He was always acting in love. Everything is rooted in love. The journey inward, into the depths of our hearts, freeing aspects of resistance and old hurts, is the most challenging yet rewarding adventure we can make. My emotional heart was too wounded to see, my ego too fragile to let go of the protective shield over my heart. This is what has been masking the Heart Cave. I see now. Oh, this love."

Twelve

The Fire of Surrender

It is the divine play in action. Love is there in our flawed human forms with our ego-driven tendencies, our busy minds, and our busy bodies. The love is there when we are unable to stop to enjoy this precious unfolding. That, too, is the play.

An Ocean of Love

E arly morning in my room, I continued the heart meditation. I could scarcely breathe, and was overcome with the sensation of being in an ocean of love. It was swallowing me up. I wrote, "Today feels freshly sweet like a lover's return. I tasted the dew and the moisture touched my lips, as I realized I have always been in the ocean of this beloved sea of the Divine. Each precious manifestation, each movement, each experience, this precious moment is all the dance of the Divine. No judgment. No error or correct action. Each emotion is part of the dance. I have been meditating on the flame, the fire in the heart. In my further initiation into this Grace, I surrendered myself into this fire."

I left Joel a question, not expecting that he would really answer it. It was titled, Stupid Question. I asked him if one could die from performing this practice. I described my sensations of either drowning in the sea of love, or feeling like I wanted to die into the divine union. I added that surrendering when the outcome is unknown called for a radical trust.

My mind was growing quieter, yet I was noticing thoughts that were arising were somehow all about me. These thoughts ranged from what I would be doing next, what I wanted, how I felt, and what I was experiencing. They also included running dialogs of past conversations, and even a narration of how I could direct attention within a meditation or spiritual experience. After a long afternoon of seeing my self-centered thoughts so plainly, I felt nearly sickened and filled with disbelief. These thoughts seemed endless! I wrote, "I am seeing the story of Cathy so clearly. Oh brother!"

The next day I wrote, "My inquiries and mediations on the heart are starting to lead me where my mind does not want to go. I am approaching a new level of surrender. A big part of me is all for the idea of surrender and is even willing to die into all of this. However, now I have hit a new level of resistance. Am I willing to surrender my life to the Divine, to Ramana, to Shiva, without knowing what the outcome will be?"

Shiva's Radiance

During the next day's session, Joel answered my question. He talked about how the intense Bhakti experiences of wanting to die into the Divine can happen, but it is not an act of self-will. The further on the Bhakti Path one travels, the more it is revealed that it is impossible to be separate from the Divine, the one Consciousness.

Later that afternoon my journal continued, "My devotion for Ramana has been unwavering for close to two years. My devotion to Shiva has been present and with me since going to India. I may not know the full experience of the Radiant Heart and how deep it may go, but it feels as though I have tapped into it. It is the current of love, and falling into the limitless space of the Heart Cave. Today, there was an incredible heart-opening experience, as I have seen all as Shiva, the Divine. While rolling up my sleeve in the dining room, I suddenly realized my body was that of Shiva. I was dressing Shiva, feeding Shiva. All was Shiva in its many manifestations, in action and inaction."

Surrendering the Bhakti Path

During our solo day we were instructed to engage in our choice of practices of the heart. Joel then described the paradox of trying to surrender. Surrender is actually impossible since, trying to surrender still stems from a delusional sense of self. He also talked about a deeper problem on this devotional path of surrender. It calls for a spiritual death, which is not where the mind wants to venture willingly. The sense of self, and objects as other than Self, including our objects of devotion, needs to pass away. Even within kenosis or the clear state, emptiness also needs to pass away, as enlightenment is no state.

Joel guided us in another meditation called Being Everything and Being a No-self. It was simple, quite sweet, and powerful. I could feel effort lift from me, then a current of love flowed through me, as a light *samadhi* state gradually swept me deeper, then deeper still, into a vast space. I immediately startled out of it. I had the thought, "There's more?" I could see clearly that all states, all experiences were arising in Consciousness, though it left me curious about the vast space I'd touched.

Where is Consciousness?

I returned to my room, and spent some time gazing at Ramana's photo, feeling an expansive heart. The question, "Where is Consciousness?" spontaneously arose, just as the dinner bell sounded. It was as though Consciousness was immediately providing all the answers. I listened to the bell fading away to silence. There were a few more light sounds of the bell, which was followed by a train whistle, a bird singing, and scratching from a ground squirrel climbing up the cabin. Consciousness continued to answer. Within seconds, the trees were glistening from a blast of sunshine and the blowing from a light gust of wind. To make sure I was receiving the message, Consciousness was revealed to include the odd sight of a little squirrel falling off the roof, past my window. The squirrel was then busy scratching its way back up the side of the cabin, as I felt my body breathing.

After dinner, I went to the meditation hall and remained for more than three hours. I used attention only to focus deeper into the heart, either by following the mantra in, or the sacred phrase of Form is Emptiness: Emptiness is Form. I searched for the self, searched after thoughts, searched for other, and searched for the boundary of myself and spacious-awareness. I invited emotions, recent struggles that seemed important. I generated self-centered thoughts to trace their origins, watching them self-liberate. I knew all, but Consciousness, to be impermanent. My journal continued, "I am empty of inherent existence. There are no boundaries of self and other except what is created within the mind. And, mind only exists in time. Consciousness is the eternal Now; it has and will be present always. In that, there is no death. In that, there is true bliss, love, and freedom."

The final morning of the retreat I awoke with the mantra being linked to my breath, then realized I was dreaming. I remained lucid as I looked into the pond at Cloud Mountain, while praying. I could feel the transition between the spiritual and Radiant Heart. When I awoke I was again saying the mantra, *Om Namo Shivaya*. The retreat ended after check-in and final chores. It was time to return home. I left feeling that somehow this retreat would stay with me. My ending prayer was noted in my journal, "Let my heart stay open to all of life. *Om Namo Shivaya*."

Thirteen

Divine Union

When we make a sincere passage into our own hearts,
Consciousness expresses itself as it will. We simply breathe
in the love that we are and allow love in.

The Flowering of Consciousness

Following the Fire in the Heart retreat I returned to work the next day. For the next week it felt as though the insights gleamed would finally carry forth. The clearest glimpses of Consciousness were noticed in the gaps between the thoughts, and the silence between sounds, even while at work. I found myself still immersed in the remembrance of the Divine. All arising and passing away was the movement of Consciousness, including my thoughts and feelings. After a day at work I wrote, "There was a witnessing of how identification with human conditioning is the source of suffering. Thoughts take us on the journey away from our true selves. Yet there can be nowhere, no thing, no situation, and no one in which Consciousness cannot be found. The silence of the open heart only seems to be growing."

The Secret of Allowing

Early November about a week following the retreat, the deepening continued. There were several dreams about meditating on the heart, then becoming lucid. One dream was about holding a red Arunachala Stone in my hand. I felt attached to it. I held the stone to my heart before giving it away to a woman I was talking to. The stone broke into three pieces. I realized that despite it being in three pieces, it was still only one.

I wrote, "Since getting back from retreat, the presence of emptiness, and the sense of being a no self has been with me. Despite all the deep meditative experiences in the past, the sense of selflessness has never taken hold before. I still haven't talked to Joel."

A pervasive sense of presence continued for another week. I remembered Joel explaining that gnostic flashes can last for hours to days to weeks, or even months, so I was still observing what was happening without becoming attached. So far, my thoughts were being held at bay and not distracting me from the Truth glimpsed during the retreat.

I then realized that love was a union with myself as myself. I was driving my car at the time and not even meditating. I described this insight further in my journal: "I suddenly realized I have never allowed love to fully be experienced within myself, as love coming from and returning to myself." Before this, it was as though I was still seeking this divine union to come from above me, and away from me, to be something that would be suddenly revealed or that would appear. This kept me waiting for the divine union to happen rather than understanding that it was always happening. It was now revealed that in allowing the flow of love to rest in the heart, this is where the divine union takes place.

I knew the Divine Consciousness is what we always and forever will be. We can never be separate from it. It is known when we are able to open into the wondrous flow of love, to fall in love with our own humanity, our own hearts. It only requires one thing from us: to simply open ourselves to receiving this love. Without reservations or holding back we fully love ourselves. This means in the midst of our lives unfolding in whatever way they do, we always return to the heart, whether in a state of contraction or expansion. I knew this to be true devotion.

This revelation of the importance of receiving love was changing my perceptions and experiences. A feeling of profound love, or a divine silence, within felt so close it was like a heartbeat within the breath. A growing understanding of some type of mysterious union was taking place. I wrote in mid-November, "There continues to be an expansive sense of presence, a silent communication or union with the sense of 'I' as the Divine. I realize it is in fully allowing love to flow back to oneself is where the meeting, the love affair resides. It is an inner dance of union, beyond bliss. Oh, in that silence, this is where true love abides, and is nourished back into itself. And, mysteriously, it has always been like this."

About a week later, I attended a conference for work called Compassionate Presence. The seminar was mostly about bringing greater mindfulness into work and life. I even saw two coworkers from the job I had left with the mental health agency before accepting my current position. There were some strained relationships when I left, particularly with one of the women attending the conference. I approached them literally saying the words, "Just showing up in presence." For one woman, it was easy for her to meet me in this space; the other woman was clearly uncomfortable. I could feel healing taking place in the space of open-heartedness. My journal continues, "It is the space where all of us naturally abide but avoid with our busy thoughts, resentments, grudges, and emotional walls of protection. In fully meeting my own heart, there is freedom."

Love Returning

We make our own hearts the focus of our devotion.
This is the secret to opening to the great Heart of
Awareness, the Radiant Heart.

Following the Compassionate Presence conference that evening I attended a community *satsang* held by David in Eugene. I had cleared my schedule in case I was drawn to attend the full weekend retreat, which I was. The first night, David taught about Advaita Vedanta, meaning not two, only One. Afterwards, I rose to talk with him. I explained that only recently did I begin to understand his advice, and explained how I had missed the importance of allowing love to return back into itself, which happens by fully opening to my own heart. It was a warm connection.

Late that evening, I sat alone in our spare room awed about where this journey has taken me. I thought about how it has all been about making a sincere passage into the heart, returning to that one Love. Allowing our own hearts to be the object of devotion seemed to hold the key to opening to the great Heart of Consciousness. I knew this was true for all humanity. It comes down to whether or not we can meet ourselves completely and honestly, and be open to the movements of Grace.

Shivananda

During the second day of the retreat, I experienced sensations during meditation that are difficult to describe. The more love was being received back into the heart, the love affair with the Divine, Shiva, was happening within me. Yet, this union was formless and timeless. I experienced the first of many floodings on a physical, emotional and spiritual level when I first heard "Shivananda" within me. It was an intense current of energy filling my body with such bliss and tenderness.

On the third day of the retreat there was more 'flooding' and a shift of perception in the boundaries of the heart. The sense of presence was expanding once more. My journal continued, "The sacred word, Shivananda continues to come to me. A devotional feeling of Shiva presented itself in a flash of union, as a tantric energy moved up my chakras. Mysteriously, my love for the Divine has returned to the heart as love for myself. The merging I once prayed for is happening. A spacious-awareness without boundaries is becoming prevalent, as though my heart is now sensing the whole Universe. The blissful floodings continue to come in like waves and are lasting long periods of time."

On the last day of the retreat I felt a timeless quality of being connected to everything and everyone. I wrote, "All resides in the Heart, how wonderful. Love is limitless when we fully open to it—It just flows in and in endlessly."

The retreat ended, but the floodings continued. These experiences were at first only limited to meditations, but soon would happen during my daily life, often several times a week. The floodings initially overwhelmed me. If I was driving, I needed to pull the car over. Tears of bliss would stream down my face, or if I would relax my eyes a *samadhi* would start to overtake me while at work.

Life continued to open to degrees I had never experienced. Boundaries were fading and the sense of my body was becoming less rigid. I was becoming the open vessel that I once meditated on. The Self was everything. This tender heart within my form was receiving the incredible beauty of life unfolding, even when there were challenges for the mind. The Heart of Consciousness was overtaking me. I knew Shivananda was a name that didn't belong to me. However, Shivananda seemed to be naming this union of myself fully opening to and receiving the love of the Divine.

Fourteen

A Shift of Gravity

The resistance we think we are experiencing out there is still only experienced inside, in the heart. There is no outside or inside. Love surrounds everything, even that which we resist. It is all a returning to the Source, this Heart of Consciousness, which is the Self.

Deepening, Beyond Mind

About a week later, and over a month following the Fire in the Heart Retreat, I wrote: "Nov. 29. The spiritual journey continues to engulf me. There have been more nights of dreamless sleep, and more opportunities to see this mind-talk as just part of the divine dance. There has been a growing sense of hollowness, of being a no self, and witnessing the inner silence deepen with more steadiness."

It then seemed like it was time to talk to Joel. I caught him up on the highlights. His only advice was to not let the mind create a story, even a spiritual story, or to become lost in the mind's movements. Joel also pointed out that everything comes from the mind even if they are spiritual thoughts. He also cautioned about not getting wrapped up or confused if there are times of dullness, when it seems nothing is happening. Instead, his advice was to look at the mind directly to where these thoughts are being generated. He ended with saying something like, "Clearly you are being led" and that ultimately he did not have any advice to give, saying, "Don't try to fix what isn't broke."

There were a few spiritual dreams around this time, which I recorded in my journal: "Dec. 4. David and several others were on a journey, leaving the Mountain. David walked alone, then others were walking alone. I was walking with different men, walking on a sandy trail with scattered rocks. We were also leaving the Mountain. The fourth man I walked with was Dai. We sat looking back at the Mountain sharing the silence. A meditative presence of great spaciousness occurred and then a *samadhi* overtook me. There was simply the union with the divine Consciousness, which included all. The words spoken between us acknowledged that there was no separation, no male or female. We were the same. We were One, and only That."

My heart continued to expand. It didn't seem to matter anymore where I was. I wrote the following after returning home from work: "I am in the heart. Mind is greatly quiet and movements of the body spontaneous. I am no longer relying on my thinking mind to figure things out. Things happen on their own. The sense of spacious presence is so vast. A dream from last night has stayed with me throughout the day. I was in a field. There were communications with Papaji[20] and Ramana, and a sense of graduating to different levels of understanding before being able to move in the field. Arunachala was in the background. I was the witness, the speaker, the listener in this meditative presence."

Bringing Spirituality to Daily Life

Just before I traveled to India again, coworkers, friends, and even family members were asking my advice about their interpersonal struggles. In a series of e-mails about opening the heart to life, I expressed this understanding, "When one lives through the open space of the heart, emotional events and challenges do not stick. They flow through. The more we discover that all is experienced within our hearts, the more we are able to be fully present to what is going on in our lives. We just feel what is going on, allowing love to be received in its many forms. Even losses, challenges, and other instances we do not understand are welcomed into the heart. Moving from the space of contraction to expansion becomes the movement of freedom."

I started sharing a few techniques, which I referred to as "The shift of gravity from the head to the heart:"

The Shift of Gravity from the Head to the Heart

1. Tune into the presence of the breath; feel the chest rising.

2. Notice if this space of the heart feels full or even achy. Know there is nothing to do and no need to change it.

3. Bring attention to the space of the heart throughout the day. Continue to feel the presence of the heart.

4. A growing willingness and acceptance to live life just as it is, is experienced. This is living with a heart of presence. The heart can take it all in, and receives by letting in.

5. Breathe into any feelings of contraction, simply resting in the space of expansion. Just be with what you are feeling, settling once more into the Heart Space. This is Freedom.

Spirituality was becoming ever present even when living my everyday life as householder. I wrote the following entries: "Dec. 20. I leave in two weeks and feel nothing is holding back within me. I am living true to the spiritual guidance that is abundant in my life, feeling the expansiveness in my heart as I go about my busy job. I no longer feel any urgency regarding whether I should be doing something different that would allow greater flexibility to write, travel, and follow my spiritual pursuits. I trust things are being taken care of, and the current of this divine love is certainly guiding me.

As I walk, I am aware that things are just happening on its own without my effort. I have no plan on how I am going to move my arms, what tree I will look at, how I will feel, or what direction my life is taking me. All I can do is be a loving witness to this beautiful unfolding. How wonderful it is to be truly alive."

"Dec. 27. Some of my coworkers have voiced they miss the old Cathy or at other times that the old, joyous Cathy is back. It does not feel like I have gone anywhere. The movement to be lively or quiet just happens spontaneously. There is no plan, no purpose, no goal, and no avoidance. There is only this mysterious unfolding."

Soon I would be traveling alone to India and spending my whole time in Tiruvannamalai, near Arunachala. The ancient city of Varanasi would have to wait for another trip, since arriving to the Sacred Mountain with an open heart was the calling.

Fifteen

The Return

Consciousness Is. Despite the appearance of traveling from place to place, and the sense of time that seems to dictate our lives, the 'I' within remains unchanged in every circumstance. In waking and dreaming, in every interaction, we are That.

The Mountain had called me back. I arrived in India shortly after the first of the year, and would be staying nearly a month. I wrote about my arrival in my journal: "It feels unreal that I am even here. The experience of traveling and changing locations from airport to airport, country to country felt like nothing was really happening. I have not changed. 'I' stays the same. Whether at work, at home, driving, or traveling (even being here in busy India), I see that this is the play and my form is a participant. It's God's Play. It's God's joy. Even the breath I take is not my own."

When I was flying to Singapore from Hong Kong I sat next to a man who was returning to India to visit his family. He made this analogy, "God is the driver and all the cars. Only God is driving, we just think we are."

Love on the Airplane

As the plane was about to land in Chennai, I was again reminded of the lessons of love. I was sitting near an American-Indian family likely returning with their baby to visit family. The baby had been quiet for the most part, but as the plane was getting ready to land she starting crying loudly. This lasted for ten to fifteen intense minutes. I was sitting next to the father who was trying to calm his little girl. The baby was often placed toward me causing my ears and head to ring with the incredible, piercing sound. I could see people in the business class section ahead of me turning around disapprovingly, and others around us scowling while others showed compassion for the child who was overly-tired and distressed.

The crying continued and only seemed to increase. I suddenly felt that this too was God, and was reminded of the disabled beggar who was put out in the street to beg. So here was the message again, only this time it came through sound, not sight. I felt the current of love, or a flooding overtake me. I breathed in the love for this child, appreciating her parent's unconditional love for her, and looked at her sweet face masked with tears.

We landed and the crying gradually grew softer and softer. Her parents were trying to distract her by pointing at the shiny airport lights, the bright red fire engines, and other airplanes. Before long, she snuggled into her daddy's arms, still breathing heavily from all her sobbing. Her daddy held her closer and closer. She looked at me, and I could feel much love coming from her. She was letting herself be consoled and comforted. I breathed in the love for her, and sent her a message: "Just let it in, let the love in." At that moment, the love completely and utterly was rushing through me, filling me. I had let in. There was no difference of the love for another. So tenderly the current of love was streaming forth from within and without. I thought if the entire world could do this there would be only peace.

Mother India's Welcome

Following this heart opening experience, I arrived in Chennai at around 10:00 p.m. Since it was my second trip I felt more at ease as I made my way through the simple, yet crowded airport. Immediately, I could see how spirituality is expressed so easily in India, something usually kept private in the States. A security officer had his forehead painted brightly with long horizontal stripes of red and white, symbolizing him as a devotee of Shiva. On my flights to get to India, and again as I was standing in line for Customs, I spotted many men wearing turbans, women wearing the typical red dots on their foreheads, showing they were likely devotees of Krishna or were Hindu. Wearing my custom-made coral and sacred *rudraksha* seed necklace, I felt like I was returning home.

It was a long, traffic-filled ride, India-Style. I was talking to the taxi driver about driving in India versus driving in America. He said that in America everyone was supposed to be in only one spot and to only travel here and there, within the area allowed to the driver. He went on to explain that in India they do not feel that space needs to be reserved for only one person. In India he said there is a free movement in and out of the whole space, it is not owned, and drivers keep watch for the gaps. It seemed that he was pointing to a deeper truth. When we become rigid about the changes occurring in life, we keep ourselves from living in the flow of life. We resist the Cosmic Dance unfolding. Instead, we can move in and out of the changes occurring by noticing the gaps or spaciousness in the midst of what is arising. There is always space if we slow down enough to look.

I arrived in Tiruvannamalai at 2:00 a.m., and was driven a short distance to the village I stayed at the previous year. I quickly settled into the room my dear friend Dai found me. It was quite nice for the price and by Indian standards. Marble floors, clean, private bathroom, ceiling fan, on the second floor, and with a partial view of Arunachala—far more than what I was expecting. Dai was also traveling in India, so once again we would be able to share some time at the Mountain. Soon after my arrival, the moon helped me glimpse a silhouetted view of the Sacred Mountain. I felt welcomed.

At 5:30 a.m. I got ready, which entailed packing a shoulder bag with water, money, camera, and a thin cushion in case I ended up meditating in a cave or stone-floored ashram. I walked on a nearby trail that meandered through a meadow. The darkness was like a blanket covering the meadow, about to be lifted by a sliver of sun low on the horizon. I could see several *sadhus* in the distance, some huddled near small fires to keep warm. The pungent smell of burnt plastic and trash was present, as were the scenes of *sadhus* using the field as their not-so private bathroom. The smoke coiling up made the morning mist look dreamy.

I quickly nicknamed the trail the Sadhu Trail, and would later learn I was staying near five ashrams. Once on the small road, locals were awake early sweeping their walks and painting decorative chalk blessings in front of their doors. Several shop owners were preparing for the day. For some this meant removing plastic tarps from their carts, for others unlocking rolling steel gates. A group of men were grouped together talking, while women were milking cows. Some beggars were still sleeping on the side of the road, nestled on pieces of cardboard.

I met Dai as planned at 6:00 for some chai at a nearby stand. We spent the next four hours walking the 8-mile loop around the

Mountain. I heard the scoop on what shops were open and closed, where I could buy a chocolate scone or a good cup of coffee. The Mountain was lush after receiving so much rain, since a record rainfall had ended only three weeks earlier. Some parts of the trail had been washed away. We dodged mud puddles, adding a bit of a challenge. However, seeing the Mountain so green and vibrant made getting my feet wet worth it.

Eventually the trail became too difficult to walk the full inner path, so we detoured to the main road that led to the lively streets of Tiruvannamalai. Walking into town after being surrounded by the serenity and beauty of the Mountain is best described as an assault on all senses. Pleasant smells from the stalls preparing food, stands selling large marigold garlands laced with jasmine were mixed with the harsher sights and smells of trash, polluted water, and the not-so-rare fecal matter. Cows with their painted horns, some with unpredictable personalities, strolled casually, sharing the road. Many stray dogs soon made their appearance, either curled up sleeping the morning away (presumably after a long night of adventure and barking), or on the go, dodging traffic at the last second.

We walked past several *sadhus* with colorful dress and painted foreheads. Some would beg or make eye contact, while a few bestowed a kind smile or Namaste greeting. The beggars were plentiful and persistent. Many had their hands out or were making eating gestures with their hands. Children with dark, bright eyes would often say hello then grab onto our clothing determined to receive their requested donation. Others would gently hold our hands and after a few moments run away giggling.

All this was mixed with the frantic horns of dashing trucks, auto rickshaws, and zooming motorcycles, potbelly pigs sifting through the trash, and giant ox with their blue-painted horns pulling overloaded carts. Local people and tourists would make eye contact curiously, often exchanging smiles. I found myself tempted to just get lost in the sights, sounds, and sensations of life passing by. However, it became quickly evident and necessary for my survival to be alert in the midst of it all. Behind me was the loud blast of a horn clearly meaning for me to get out of the way!

My journal entry described my impressions of my first day in India: "Being in India is an invitation to join in the culture, starting with dodging traffic like the roaming dogs. There is an immediate sense of being in the play of it all. It is difficult—if not impossible to just to be a spectator in this lively culture. This is India. May we keep our hearts open to it all!"

Using the laptop Steve bought me for Christmas, I worked on my first spiritual book, "Bringing Home the Mountain." I brought along four journals that gave a detailed account of my spiritual path and my hidden spiritual pride (not so hidden from my teachers, Joel and David). I was finding it an interesting process, since the first draft that was started a year earlier primarily focused on all of my flowery spiritual experiences. Two weeks before my second trip to India I started adding journal entries that were for my eyes only. I believed that if this book were to be helpful to others, sharing my spiritual struggles needed to also be included.

On my third morning I attended Shiva Shakti's public *darshan*. I showed up with an open heart and open mind. When I looked at her, I realized that we were both the same. As soon as this thought arrived, she gave me a sweet smile then zapped me into a *samadhi* state. My heart felt full and my eyes locked shut for some time even though I wanted to see her again. I felt gratitude that she helped me open my heart during my last visit. I planned to return for evening *darshan*, however beyond this next visit I likely would not see her much. My work with Shiva Shakti felt done.

The Garland of the Heart

Later that afternoon I was surprised to find myself walking to the Ramanasramam instead of going back to see Shiva Shakti as I had planned. I sat on the cool, black, stone floor in the Old Hall looking at Ramana's life-sized photograph that rests on his old couch. Soon after, chanting came from the adjoining hall that contains a tomb housing Ramana's remains. The chanting seemed to vibrate through me as I continued to look into Ramana's eyes. I ended up at Ramana's Samadhi Hall where the *puja* was in full force. I joined others to walk around the elevated platform, which houses a statue of Ramana, and a lotus-shaped stand and lingam placed over his tomb. Two rows of Brahman men and boys were chanting. I then entered the Mother Shrine where I knew I would find the beloved Dancing Shiva statue. I noticed how they had replaced the leopard pants that the Shiva statue was wearing during my last visit with some colorful cloth. A few garlands of fresh flowers were placed carefully over the circle of dancing arms.

I walked in the darkened Mother Shrine several times paying homage to the many statues with their individual candles and small fire offerings. I stopped to gaze into the open doors containing the inner sanctum, which is considered an empowered place of devotion that contains the remains of Ramana's mother. Antique brass lights hang in the darkness of the inner sanctum lending it a mysterious and sacred aura. A ritual taking place drew me in further as I watched two Brahman priests prepare the inner sanctum for viewing. Most people were in the Samadhi Hall so the Mother Shrine was otherwise quiet. Chanting could be heard from the other room, adding another layer to the mystique and warmth that was overtaking me.

The priest was washing all the statues and inner shrine by pouring buckets of water over the statues. I had never seen this before and was moved to stay and watch. Others continued to enter and walk around the inner shrine. I had now stopped to stand near a large, sacred cow statue watching the purification ceremony and cleansing of the inner sanctum. I recognized the inner sanctum to be a representation of the inner heart, the cave of the sacred heart. With this understanding I felt a flooding of the outer world being within my heart. All was this Heart. The activities of cleansing this inner sanctum were now felt inside my heart. My heart was thumping and felt expansive as it was being cleansed with the water, then purified and blessed with sacred milk that was being poured over each of the carefully-tended statues. Then more water was poured over the statues as my heart was further purified and cleansed. The priest went on to dry the statues, then carefully dress them with clean colorful cloth.

The final step was for the priest to adorn all the inner sanctum statues with garlands and single flowers. They were adorning my heart after it had been cleansed and fully accepted. It was such a blessing and a feeling of love as I allowed my heart to be adorned with the flowers and garlands. I went back to the Dancing Shiva statue. Now there were small oil containers burning for each temple deity. I allowed this purification and blessing of the heart to continue and ended my time there by waving my right hand over the flame (as my Hindu grandmother had taught me last trip), feeling the warmth then inviting the fire of Shiva into my heart. I knew this all to be the blessing of the garland of the Heart.

Darshan is Everywhere

The next morning I awoke to the sound of a dog barking. Although it was 4:00 a.m., I couldn't help but laugh. The barking sounded like it was laughing and talking. I thought of Ramana's sense of humor. I meditated lying in bed before getting up formally to meditate, yet this implies too much effort. Meditation had become *darshan,* or simply being in the present moment. I was reminded of Tom McFarlane's teaching of being an empty vessel. This seemed to best describe the growing sense I experienced in meditation and in daily life. My journal described this further: "I am experiencing more and more how everything around me is taking place without me doing anything. All of life is unfolding perfectly in the great landscape of Awareness. I was looking at Ramana's photo, which I placed on an altar beside my bed. While gazing into Ramana's eyes his smiling face intrigued me, as a feeling of his timeless love, acceptance, and even humor was present. I wondered if whether receiving *darshan* while looking at Ramana's photograph was possible. Then, as though the question was instantly answered, I understood that all was *darshan* as we experience everything in our hearts."

I felt inspired to visit Ramana's lower cave, my first journey there since returning. On my way it seemed that everything that was arising was a blessing of *darshan*. It didn't seem to matter what it was: the big red butterfly, trash strewn on the roadside, a persistent vendor, a smiling face, or a stray dog. All was *darshan*. Feeling a full heart, I entered the cave. The crowded cave quickly reminded me that it was a Hindu holy day. I was unable to sit in my favorite area, the inner chamber that houses a sacred lingam.

Instead, I sat in the outside chamber of the cave. I was breathing in the love of being back in this sacred place, looking at several portraits of Ramana that decorate the walls. My heart was taking in the energy of everything swirling around me, primary the volume of people coming in and out of the cave making their pilgrimage. I could sense that a woman holding a child kept looking at me, and would occasionally whisper to her friends who were sitting nearby. Before long she came over to place her baby in my arms and made a gesture of wanting a blessing. I just held the baby with love. After awhile she took the baby from me and smiled. I left after they did but caught up with them up the hill. They had stopped to have a picnic on a cliff that overlooked the city temple. The woman smiled at me, then approached me to ask my name. I nearly said, "Shivananda" but the words didn't come. I then said "Cathy." We exchanged warm Namaste greetings as I left. A powerful feeling that everything was unfolding perfectly, and it was all *darshan*, continued the rest of the day. My journal entry described the insight that carried forth: "All we have to do is be present in the heart, then the gift of Grace, of *darshan* comes freely and unceasingly. Receiving and giving is the same. It is all Love. It is all *darshan*."

Learning that the *sadhu* that tends Ramana's upper cave chants each morning, I left my room before 7:00 a.m. the next morning to hear him. As it was too early to take a short cut through the Ramanasramam, I walked in the early morning light on the Sadhu Trail to the main road, to the rear of the Hindu Shrine and Ashram, past the gazing pool, to the rear of the Ramanasramam, then began my walk up to the cave. Although I was walking faster than normal I was mindful that everything I was seeing and experiencing was *darshan*. *Darshan* was experienced in any physical discomfort, the blue lizard, and the pink hue in the sky. *Darshan* was the *sadhu's* melodic chanting, the prayers, and offerings of incense and flowers that quickly adorned the cave.

As I left the *sadhu,* I recognized his silence as *darsh*an, along with the Asian woman who was weeping, utterly lost in devotion. *Darshan* continued with meeting the Flower Sadhu as he joyously chanted to me, "*Om Shiva Shakti Om, Om Shivaya.*" He then gave me a rose and painted my forehead with sacred ash. Off the hill, *darshan* continued in its many manifestations. Even those who stared without returning my smile, and the female beggar demanding a donation, this too was *darshan*. Back on the Sadhu Trail I felt the presence of the Mountain inside my heart. I then gave *darshan* to my beloved Shiva in the form of the Mountain, gazing deeply then sending a transmission of love. All I could feel was the love returning in full force. I closed my eyes as I relaxed into a *samadhi*. It was then that I realized that *darshan* is only possible in the receiving. *Darshan* is love returning back into itself from the Self. This is the blessing of *darshan*.

PART VI:

Searching Beyond Experience

Sixteen

Mind Creeping In

*The biggest trickster that so often convinces us that we are
not already awake is our own thoughts. Yet, these thoughts
we may think we possess or control are arising in
Consciousness, just as much as our spiritual experiences.*

My first five days in India passed with a full heart, and Grace was abundant once more. The journey into the Self only continued. I was increasingly aware of what I was seeing in the outer world was truly a reflection of what was happening inside me. Despite this wonderful return to India, on the sixth day I found that there was a sudden increase in thoughts. In fact, once again, my mind was busy causing havoc. For the first time in several months I was starting to become lost amid the dream of being a separate self. I felt ownership of the individual thoughts arising, and tried to control them, which of course, in turn only seemed to increase their seductive powers.

I was feeling less and less enlightened by the moment.

Mind Creeping Out . . .

In the evening I listened to a spiritual teaching by Adyashanti on my iPod. It was a perfect fit for what my mind was posing as a problem. Adyashanti described how it would be more accurate to say we are 'egoing' rather than that there is an ego. He also talked about it being impossible to rid ourselves of thoughts, so to hold onto this goal is futile. I added to my journal, "So, the mind/ego is just a movement of thought. When we follow the movement of our minds with our attention, we give our thoughts meaning, which we then connect to who we think we are. This gives us the impression of having a separate identity. Yet, this show of the mind is all arising on its own. It is all a part of Consciousness. Anger is only anger. Confusion is only confusion. We name this movement of energy, whether it is anger or confusion by the act of labeling, which the mind is adept at. However, it is not a person's anger or confusion. It belongs to no one unless the mind decides to claim ownership, and that, paradoxically, does not even exist either."

Morning Blessing

I planned to meet Dai for a morning walk around the Mountain, but woke up experiencing the consequences of eating something that didn't agree with me. I figured it would be a good opportunity to spend the day writing in my journal and meditating. However, I met him at our regular chai stand as planned to let him know I would not be joining him. Dai encouraged me to allow the stillness to take over. We were discussing this when our attention was drawn to something in the distance. An elderly man was coming towards us from the darkened street. He had a long thin, white beard, a cane, and was dressed in all white, except for a pale brown shawl draped over one shoulder. Dai appeared to know him. I made a gesture to invite him to join us for a cup of chai.

He greeted us kindly but declined our offer of tea. Soon he asked me if this was my first trip to India. I responded that it was my second trip. Holding my hand to my heart, I said that Arunachala was special. He voiced kindly, "Arunachala roots out the ego, and the Mountain is very magnetic." The man gazed at both of us then said we were all already free and to not be concerned about the ego, that we were not our bodies, nor our thoughts, and that none of that mattered. We were the Self, Ramana, and the Mountain. I soon recognized this man to be the Saint that Dai had mentioned meeting recently. The Saint is known as K.V.C. due to his long name. He reportedly met Ramana when he was a boy, before Ramana's death. The Saint smiled humbly as he left us placing his hands over his heart in prayer. Soon after, Dai and I both acknowledged this as an incredible blessing.

While standing on the Sadhu Trail on the way back to my room, the Mountain's energy felt expansive. It seemed to be calling me to simply be present in stillness. I faced the Mountain feeling the wind and a giant opening beginning in my heart. The Mystery was overtaking me, along with any ideas of what I should be doing. I do not know how long I stood there. I was aware of *sadhus*, people, school children on bikes, and dogs occasionally passing by. Dragonflies and butterflies appeared, some seemed to dance around me before fluttering down the trail. Unusual birds with their bright colors were singing beautiful melodies. The Mountain's presence was encompassing it all.

Reflections on the Mind

As I closed another day in India, I wrote the following in my journal: "I danced freely on the roof this late afternoon, as I gazed at the dazzling view of Arunachala. I knew the Mountain and I to be One. I continue to feel the loving transmission from the Mountain, an openness of being in the present moment that is fresh and mysteriously innocent. Self-inquiry continues to be my main meditation practice. I continue to drive attention deeper into the heart to find the source of the Self, the 'I.' It is to exhaust the search, to know for sure if I have found Truth. This is in response to my busy mind introducing doubt, raising questions about whether I have truly gone deep enough into the heart. These are the ramblings of the mind."

I awoke the next morning with the words "Arunachala Shiva" on my mind. It seemed I had been practicing a mantra in my dreams. After meditating, I pondered a quote from the *Words of Sri Anandamayi Ma*. Anandamayi Ma, known as the Mother of Bliss, was a twentieth-century Hindu saint. Our group at the Center was studying her teachings when I left, so I brought a booklet of her teachings along as homework. I randomly selected a verse while gazing at Ramana's photo. The following verse is what came. However, at first I did not like it too much. I closed the book to find another more suitable teaching. The same quotation immediately revealed itself despite my efforts to suppress it:

> *Is peace possible in the domain of want? Ever new*
> *desires will arise. Sense objects only generate poison*
> *but never give real peace. Caught in the round of*
> *coming and going, can one be at peace? As long as*
> *there are two, there will be sorrow. Duality breeds*
> *conflict, pain. Sorrow arises from want. So long as*
> *you are not established in your true being you cannot*
> *be at peace.*[21] *~Sri Anandamayi Ma*

Sri Anandamayi Ma's words seemed to point to a truth based on simplicity, namely the present moment. After focusing on the last verse, I wrote the following, "There is a simple, but profound recognition that true being is only possible in present moment awareness. Again, my confusion is simply the cause of following my thoughts. It is by wanting some endpoint of understanding that takes me away from just being with this Mystery now."

As I was reflecting on my recent confusion, I contributed it to reading a passage from *No mind, I am the Self*[22] by David Godman, about the teachings of Sri Lakshmana Swamy. A student described how a self-inquiry practice leads to experiencing that there is no mind, then a feeling of emptiness. Sri Lakshmana Swamy asked the student if he is not the mind who experiences emptiness. He told the student that all of his questions and experiences are still coming from the mind, and that he should ask, "Who experiences emptiness? Who thinks he is not the mind?"

Sitting with my confusion, I allowed myself to nap while being mindful of my heart center and the question, "Who am I?" I then drifted into a dream. The dream was of me rising from my bed and walking around my room. I became lucid and touched the wall. There was no difference between the self of my experience, and what I was experiencing as the Self (Consciousness). I then inquired into where the source of attention was by driving attention into my heart space, then suddenly just relaxed. It was as though everything melted into a sense of pure being.

After a day of meditating, I wrote the following: "I have been inquiring into what experience really is. Experiencing this present moment, this mysterious void is all I know. If experience is an obstacle to true understanding then I am certainly getting stuck in the experience aspect of it all." Immediately, as I was writing this, I knew I was muddying the waters by trying to go deeper into the experience of the Source. I continue in my journal, "The sense of emptiness has been revealed already. I know that attention always returns to the Source, and that everything arises from the Source. I am, again, chasing after a tail that does not exist. I see the futility of my efforts. There is nothing for me to do except to let Grace guide me deeper. I am already here and live in this unchanging state. My thoughts are thoughts, and nothing more than that. The flow of thoughts does not change this presence of Truth."

I sent off an e-mail titled, "Calling my Spiritual Teachers . . . Busy mind alert!" I invited Joel, Tom Kurzka, and a few others from the Center to respond with any feedback, if they felt moved to do so. There was a deep knowing that my own mind was just tripping me up, but there was still the question about my experiences of awakening. Did this mean that all experiences were generated from the mind, but the insights were coming from the Source? My mind was settling, but I still had questions about Swamy's teachings.

I walked around the Mountain the next morning. I recognized how the movements of past and future thinking is what keeps the momentum of the mind going, but our thoughts are not real. They flitter in and out, yet have no substance, and are always changing. As I walked, I was aware of these movements of thoughts, which we label as mind. It is through remembering past events and future thinking that the sense of an individual identity is possible. I knew that by returning to the Source with the breath or with attention residing in the heart, Truth is revealed.

Later, after checking my e-mails, I received a response from Tom Kurzka regarding the 'busy mind alert' email I sent: "Hi Cathy, Source cannot be grabbed and held onto. Hence, the teaching that in every moment there is the choice, to follow the mind (and experience), or fall back into Source. Even the tasting of this Source is an experience. Source is only Source, and that is why it is called a 'Mystery.' So no matter what is arising, fall back into the Source. You are past the point of explanation and words. You are past the point of experience, no matter how profound. Be still. Fall back into the Source. Expect nothing. You know this already. Give up the journals, the writing, and the computer; these all get the mind going. You are in India. Be still. Fall back into the Source all day long. This is why you are in India. You are not there to write. There will be plenty of time to write and think and process when you are back in the U.S."

The Flower Within the Heart

Despite thinking I would begin my time of silence in a few days, early that evening I went to the little store to buy supplies to start a solo retreat. I planned to not stray far from my room, if at all. I would use some of my reading material for meditation and self-inquiry, helping to structure my time.

I began the day with reflecting on the Anandamayi Ma verse I chose earlier. The verse suddenly revealed the whole spiritual path, and why it is so difficult to move beyond this story of me. I could see how want or desire arises so often: to want a new posture, to want the bug to stop crawling on me, wanting more tea or something to eat, wanting greater understanding, or a focused mind. Thus, the only lasting peace is That which is unchanging. Wanting or desire is the movement away from what is here right now. It is moving away from the gift of this moment, and a denial of the perfection of the

Infinite. Suffering does not exist in the present moment, only in the movements away from presence.

I wrote in my journal, "Allowing the Divine play to unfold is freedom. When all is seen as a manifestation in Consciousness, including this form and any thoughts that may arise, there is no suffering. There is no separation. Not trusting the presence of the Divine in all things, at all times, leads to suffering. Abiding in this present moment is where Divinity reveals itself."

By the afternoon, I started a powerful meditation practice based on another teaching by Sri Lakshmana Swamy from *No Mind, I am the Self*[23] by David Godman. The instructions are to follow the "Who am I?" question even deeper by catching where the individual I-thought, or thought about the personal self, first resides then tracing it back to its Source. By doing so, the Source is discovered to be the Self (Consciousness), which all arises from and passes away. By catching hold of the I-thought, the Self will then devour it. The ego will then rest in the Self and be as harmless as a burned rope.[24]

Several questions were arising as I read the teaching from Sri Lakshmana Swamy. So, I meditated on several self-inquiry questions: Where is the source? Who is thinking? Is the source other than the heart? Where are the boundaries of the heart space? I then followed the instructions described in Swamy's meditation, which I continued to engage in throughout the day, even when not meditating. I followed the I-thought budding or in full splendor to the source, the Heart. This meant staying alert to any thoughts I was having about myself, what I thought, what I wanted, or what I was experiencing. My goal was to see where this sense of myself arose, and place my attention there. Because these thoughts were often arising quickly, I clung to the tail of the I-thought, so it could not escape. (Another way to describe this for those who are familiar with thoughts self-liberating is to follow the thought to the point where it ceases to exist, but to hold attention intensely on it until there is absolutely no residue or energy left of the thought.) Sometimes, other I-thoughts would arise while I was holding onto one thought. I grabbed hold of them also, absorbing all into the heart. All returned to the Source, which is the Self.

This practice was sometimes exhausting, as this process would repeat itself over and over for hours. Towards the end it seemed that no thoughts were truly arising. It became only a subtle movement that I was following, then pulling back any arising thought with attention back into the heart. The heart became incredibly expansive and developed an aching sensation of feeling too full. After awhile, I discovered that pulling the I-thought took no effort at all, and that simply following the breath back to the heart space was enough and completed this same task.

I deliberately avoided following bliss or other experiences that could distract me from abiding in the emptiness of the heart space. At one point an image manifested despite the avoidance of following anything other than the I-thoughts. It was an image or vision of the heart appearing in my mind's eye. A surreal sense of the heart, almost a bluish, purple color grew and surrounded my body. An erasing process then started in one spot, and continued around my whole body until there were no longer boundaries of any kind of the heart. A tiny red flower appeared as though it was being handed to me. It seemed that something inside of me accepted the flower. It was placed in my own heart and represented all hearts, the Heart of Consciousness.

After this lengthy meditation, it was sunset. I gazed at the Mountain. The Mountain was within, and without. Everything was within, and also without. I added the following to my journal, "The Heart resides everywhere and is timeless. Its location is not limited to the physical realm or in time; it is the Mystery, the Source."

The next morning I awoke from a vivid dream. It was about a fantastic craving to ride a horse. (I am not a horse person since getting injured as a child.) Yet in my dream I rode the horse without a saddle with complete trust feeling the wind, the warmth of the horse, and the freedom of surrender.

I then started my meditation, and the self-inquiry questions spontaneously deepened. I was left to question the accuracy that experiences only come from the mind. I wrote the following, "It is all just experience, but still a manifestation of Consciousness. Things are happening on their own."

While meditating, I saw an image of gray smoke, which turned into a cobra on my bed. The smoke and cobra became one, then started crawling up and circling my body before releasing me like the wind. *Om Shiva.*

I broke silence the next morning. I was simply gazing at the Mountain eating an orange, and then felt the urge to re-enter the world. As I walked on the Sadhu Trail on my way to send off an e-mail, a big red butterfly flew beside me the whole length of the walk. I passed by some *sadhus*. One wanted to talk. I continued to walk knowing that all I was seeing and experiencing was the manifestation of the Divine. I waited patiently for a computer, then sent off a few meditation instructions, and announced to Steve, Dai, and my teachers that I had broke silence.

My journal described my conclusions following the solo retreat: "Nothing has changed regarding my awareness and dwelling in the Source. The shift of gravity happened long ago with the awareness residing in the core of my heart. If there is a deeper recognition of this it will certainly manifest over time, as it has nothing to do with me. I am here now in this experience. I can meditate on returning to the Source, write or not write, think or not think, talk or be silent; however, these things have nothing to do with me as a separate identity. It is all the movement of Consciousness, the Divine itself."

Regarding my breaking silence, my friend Dai sent me a note: "I think Tom would say breaking the silence is not staying with the stillness within. Journaling, etc. takes you back to holding onto your experiences and as Tom said, you are beyond trying to create and hold on to more experiences. Go to the Source and stay put! Be still and know that I am God."

I added to my journal, "Of course, he makes good points, and there is the possibility that I am completely deluded. However, I am left feeling it is time to trust my own knowing. The Source is present no matter what I am doing. Times of outward silence are important, but there seems to be a point on the path that inner dwelling is always happening, no matter what is going on."

Seventeen

The Source and the Pinhole

*By probing into the Source of 'I' an understanding that there
are no true boundaries from outside, inside, self, and other is
revealed. All is this Heart.*

Getting Real with Silence

After another morning spent in Ramana's lower cave, I went to
have *darshan* with Shiva Shakti, where I felt her loving
transmission coming in waves. Back in my room, I meditated based
on teachings from a small booklet titled *The Spiritual Heart,
Bhagavan Ramana Answers*[25] by A.R. Natarajan. Ramana Maharshi
talked about there being "a small pinhole" in the spiritual heart that
remains closed until one enters into a *samadhi* state called *kevala
nirvikalpa*. This pinhole is said to open briefly, giving the person a
gnostic understanding or experience of awakening (what Joel called
a gnostic flash). However, when this pinhole opens for good, the
"knot of ignorance" is untied permanently.

These words did not make any sense. I questioned whether the
pinhole was simply a metaphoric teaching, or if it could exist. There
was also mention of the 'I'-'I.' I could not understand this either, or

why was it called, 'I'-'I' rather than 'I,' which I knew to be the Self. All these teachings were confusing. Yet, at the same time, there was an intuitive trust in their accuracy. I believed the methods of self-inquiry, abiding in the heart space, catching hold of the I-thought before its conception, and following back the I-thought to its Source would be where these teachings would be revealed. I wondered if this was where the entry point to the pinhole was located, and if I had already touched upon it. My best guess is the 'I' was the spiritual heart, and the 'I'-'I' was describing the Radiant Heart. The teaching seemed to be pointing to something that was paradoxically beyond experience, yet seemed to be encouraging just another experience in order to see what would be revealed. Nonetheless, I decided to give it a try.

Slipping into the Hole

In the center of the Heart Cave, Self shines alone. It is the form of the Self experienced directly as 'I'-'I.' Enter the Heart merging through self-inquiry or by breath-control and become rooted as That.[26]
~Bhagavan Sri Ramana Maharshi

I began meditating on the Source as I had been doing earlier, following the origins of where the I-thought arises. My mind was clear, and before long, I again was following the subtle movements of the mind with my attention. Any movement, and I directed attention back to the heart space. A *samadhi* soon took over, and I was gradually losing bodily awareness, yet my attention was bright with clarity. Soon, my attention was naturally abiding in the glowing radiance of my own heart. I had found the 'I'-'I.'

Although similar to the 'I' that I knew to be the Self, there was an absolute clarity and a feeling of a vibrant heart center. Soon, I felt a sensation of freefalling into the heart space, something which at other times I have startled out of. Then a visual tunnel appeared, the same as I have seen in dreamless sleep and in other deep meditations. This time what was revealed could best be described as a mysterious pinhole. A stream of energy was pulling any sense of myself deeper into this space. The thought then came, "What is this?" My attention did not follow the thought, nor did an answer come. Instead, my attention simply rested there. When the meditation ended spontaneously, my thoughts had stopped. Spacious-awareness of the Radiant Heart was all there was.

I then walked the Sadhu Trail through the vibrant meadow. I felt keenly alive and connected to everything. I made my way to the Old Hall where I meditated for the next hour and a half. Each breath was alive with a sensation of unity. I was the breath and all arising. All was the Heart of Consciousness. My journal described this further: "It seems that I have touched upon the natural way of being, without thoughts getting in the way. I now know the Radiant Heart to be the same as the Heart Cave, call it the 'I'-'I' or by any another name; it is all the same. There are deepening states in Consciousness, but it is all the same Awareness. It is simply the Heart, the Self, experienced with clarity beyond the division of separateness. It only takes a willingness to surrender to the pull of this Love. With each breath we can know the unchanging awareness of our hearts moment by moment."

True Devotion

The next morning I walked around the inner path of the Mountain. Soon, after leaving the trail, I came upon an unusual scene of a spiritual pilgrim. A man was completing the eight-mile loop around the Mountain by rolling his body on the road the whole way. Circumambulating the Mountain is considered a potent spiritual practice and walking the route barefoot is common. However, I opt to keep my sandals on when I walk, as do the majority of Western spiritual tourists that come to the Mountain.

This man had obviously been rolling for a while. He was already covered with abrasions, blood, and bandages, despite his friend who was ahead of him sweeping debris from the road with an oversized broom. His friend's sweeping also helped to alert the passing traffic of ox carts, motor vehicles of all types, and other pedestrians so the man could avoid serious injury. It was a spectacular demonstration of true devotion for the Mountain.

But really, I wondered what constitutes true devotion? Outward acts are only a reflection of what is going on inside the heart. All outward activities are inconsequential, as devotion is the inner journey into the Heart, the Source. (Later, I would learn that this man was likely rolling around the Mountain in remembrance of a loved one who died, as later I witnessed a man and woman rolling around the Mountain following a funeral procession.)

Nobody There

I spent the afternoon meditating in Ramana's Old Hall. The energy in the hall felt calm. There was a sense of emptiness, which I attributed to the number of people all meditating together. I slipped quickly into a *samadhi*, and the sense of losing bodily awareness started to take over. My eyes were closed then spontaneously opened. I saw a man staring intently at me from across the room. It was as if there was no he, no me. There was just awareness. We continued to look at each other seemingly both tuning into this reflection of the Divine, this same Self. The meditation deepened, then became simply a sense of presence. It was no longer anything unusual or any special state. All was unfolding in the presence of now. I was not sure if I was awake or dreaming, especially with the magical experience of looking at the man. I touched the floor of the ashram and waited with interest to see if I was dreaming, since everything seemed so surreal. The meditation then became a spontaneous breathing of surrender. Each breath I surrendered deeper into the Mystery, the Source. The movement was effortless, unlike the drawing of attention to go deeper (as I had been doing in earlier meditations).

With another day in India ending, I wrote the following in my journal: "Despite all the meditative experiences, I feel the same. There has not been any major shift in awareness or anything else tangible. The only thing observable is that there is not a strong sense of separateness, this is melting away and being seen through. I am seeing my thoughts as just thoughts, 'Cathy' as just this play in Consciousness. I see the mask, the game, and the role. Boundaries are becoming less rigid, between sleep and waking, between other and myself, and even the location of the Heart. This body is seen with greater insight; it is not permanent, there is no solid boundary. I know the Self to be everything, all manifested and unmanifested. I am no other than That. *Om*."

Eighteen

A Witness in India

*The Source is where everything comes from and returns. All
is the movement of love,
which so often is beyond the comprehension of the mind.
This love has intelligence, and leads us ever
deeper into our own hearts.*

During my remaining days in India, there were many scenes that inspired a story. My spiritual journey was no longer simply about the times spent in meditation, or visiting empowered places such as the Mother Shrine, Ramana's caves, his meditation halls, or visiting Shiva Shakti. It seemed everywhere, every day, I was encountering potent lessons.

Mine! All Mine!!!

A homeless couple who I had been donating to regularly began fighting one day. Before this, while sitting on the roadside at the end of the Sadhu Trail, they would greet me daily. I particularly liked the husband who has a deformed hand and kind eyes. I had given him five rupees the day before their squabble. I noticed his wife seemed irritated that I did not give the rupees to her. I imagined they would share it, so I didn't say anything. The next day, I planned to give another five rupees. Yet again, I felt drawn to hand the money to the husband, since it seemed that we shared more of a heart connection. I also felt a bit sorry for him, because his wife not only argued with him, but sometimes hit him.

When she realized that I was going to give the money to him again, she thrust her palm toward me, demanding that the donation be given to her. I complied, thinking she would share it with him. She then made a hoarding gesture as if to protect her money, like she was not going to share it, or even show him the amount. I left, walking toward my room not thinking much more of it, until the humor struck me about fifteen minutes later. I found myself laughing out loud, recalling about how many times that I wanted, desired, craved, or demanded. I caught my expression in the mirror. I then made a growly face to exaggerate this understanding, and rubbed my hands together like a shrewd miser, saying, "It's mine! All mine!"

The Inner Shrine

I spent another afternoon in the Mother Shrine, and caught the end of the cleansing and blessing ceremony. It was the same ceremony that I had witnessed during the Garland of the Heart experience. I felt compelled to stand still and watch the final aspects of the ceremony, which included drying off the Shiva *lingam* in the inner shrine, and draping it with clean cloth and flowers. Again, it felt as though it was my own heart that was being blessed. My heart immediately started beating hard, as though a deep, primal rhythm was penetrating my body. Bliss was ever present.

A *samadhi* took over, although I was still aware of my body and physical surroundings. I made my way out of the sacred darkness of the Mother Shrine, and looked for a place to sit in the Samadhi Hall next door. I was planning to gaze at my favorite photo of him, but it was too crowded. Instead, I went outside to sit in the front courtyard. I watched two barefoot toddlers playing, while their parents kept a protective eye. There was a feeling of expansive love. Everything that was arising in the courtyard was so clearly revealed to be a manifestation of Consciousness. Whether within the shrine or in the sunshine watching children, whether meditating or not, it was all the same. As I walked back to my room, the present moment felt radiant and pulsing with energy. That night I went to sleep sensing my heart space, each breath seemed to reveal the beauty and simplicity of life.

My sixteenth day began with a vivid dream. A *sadhu* was poking my eyes deeply by pressing his thumbs into the corners by my nose. I became completely lucid. I had dissolved, and did not have a face or head. Yet, there was total awareness. Then, another *sadhu* poked my arm and my body started to dissolve. Still there was awareness, no form needed.

The Lonely Child

Dai invited me to attend a celebration he was involved with, called the Shanti Clean-Up Project for Arunachala. A normally quiet road toward the west of the village was now bustling with giggling and ecstatic children, a score of volunteers, and proud parents. The following day the children would be removing trash while they walked up Arunachala. Fifty or so children were there when I arrived, although it was a little girl about three who caught my eye. Later, images of her would continue to pull at my heart. I surmised she lived nearby and had walked over to see what was going on. She was obviously poor, wearing only a torn and dirty shirt, and didn't appear to have any parents nearby. This was in contrast to the majority of the other children who participated in the event.

The girl observed the activities but didn't participate in the face painting, or art that was going on around her. Instead, I noticed how she would continually pick at her lower back. Several spots of blood were forming on her shirt. When she lifted up her shirt, I noticed she had several large wounds that appeared to be infected. The smell of her blood and possibly infection even attracted a passing dog that stopped to smell, and nose her back. At this, the little girl became increasingly aware of her wounds and started to cry. She held her back, hunched over like a tiny old woman as she walked barefoot to the dirt alleyway. The homes visible were mostly hay-covered sheds, and likely one of these was her home. She passed by a grandmother type sitting on a neighboring porch; she only hollered something at the child. There was no comfort or help for this little one. She went around another corner never to be seen again. I breathed in love and sent it her way. All I could do was feel love and compassion, releasing these feelings to her. My heart felt tender and full just holding her in presence. It was all I could do for her.

All Things Provided

I rose early the next morning, and planned to walk on the Mountain before meditating in Ramana's lower cave. However, I discovered I had lost my meditation cushion, likely at the Ramanasramam the night before. I decided to go there first to see if I could perhaps find it. I meditated a short while in the Old Hall. There were several people present so it was difficult to tell if the cushion was there and if someone was sitting on it. After paying homage to the Mother Shrine, the large Shiva statue, and to Ramana Maharshi's *lingam*, I went to the office to find out if they had a Lost and Found.

There was no one staffing the front office, but I spotted an elderly gentleman in the back. I knocked on the screen door, and was motioned to come in and offered a chair. The man had a gentle, knowing presence. I guessed that he must be the president or someone closely associated with the inner workings of the Ashram, and an obvious serious devotee of Ramana. There was such kindness in his eyes and his demeanor. The brief words of our conversation about my misplaced cushion were irrelevant. I knew I had been blessed by merely being in his loving presence. I waited for a short time in case the front office staff returned, since the man had suggested that I ask about lost and found items. I decided to go to Ramana's lower cave and check back later, but also realized that the cushion was not worth bothering with too much.

Arriving at the cave, I discovered one of the traditional woven mats along with a padded cushion was available, which is often rare when there are several visitors. I smiled recognizing how I was being provided an even more comfortable cushion than the one I had lost. I realized too that all my needs were being met, all was in perfect synchronicity, and were the workings of the Divine.

Who is Hurting More?

Returning to the main road after leaving the Mountain, I passed the Saint K.V.C. drinking tea with another gentleman. He smiled at me and mentioned Dai's name, as if to acknowledge that I was Dai's friend. I closed my hands in prayer to my heart feeling his blessing. No words came other than a sense of love and gratitude. I walked away, my awareness resting in the heart space. After my brief blessing from the Saint, I witnessed an unusual scene.

As I approached the guesthouse where I was staying, I heard a child's loud cries and a woman yelling. I came upon a woman holding a large stick and making threatening gestures at a girl who was perhaps eight years old. The girl was trying to hide behind a slender tree to avoid being beaten by the woman I assumed was her mother. They were speaking, likely in Tamil, the language mostly spoken in this region of southern India. I could only guess what was going on. The girl's face was red and full of tears, and from her clothing and how dirty she was, I could tell she was likely very poor. I soon surmised that the stick the woman was holding was for tending the goats that were loose in a neighboring lot. Possibly, the girl was trying to avoid the rest of some punishment that was owed to her. I did not know.

Their standoff continued but I could not tell who was louder, the mother or child. I walked past them, not avoiding their faces. I walked up to the balcony and looked over again witnessing this interaction. The mother's face was at times smiling, as she continued to taunt and tease the child, in what I could only consider to be in a sarcastic and ruthless manner. She would occasionally lunge at the child with the stick that would predictably result in the child screaming and crying fearfully. I peered at the mother's face and listened to her anger.

She was clearly suffering just as much as the child. She was just as engaged in this interaction as the child. They both wanted something and were not getting their needs met. I walked past them about a half hour later. The girl was standing in a corner of the lot looking at her mother's back, still appearing upset and rejected but no longer crying. The goats continued to graze happily on the grasses and the high thistle bushes. The sun was shining and there was a light breeze in the air. The mother sat on the ground and looked at me. I could see that she was not happy, not pleased with herself, even though she'd won this battle of wills with her daughter. And, the stick rested against the brick wall.

I thought about the many times in my life when it seemed justified to push my point of view, or to win an argument. I could remember being the hurt child, but also in the position of the now regretful mother. It was all seen as the same, just an expression of pain—yet, it was still all a movement of Consciousness, no matter the roles we play.

All is One

I returned to the Ramanasramam in the late afternoon to meditate in the Old Hall, and to look for my missing cushion. No luck and no cushions available to sit on. I sat on the stone floor for about twenty minutes, never feeling the urge to move fast enough to claim a cushion, or a better seat when they would come available. I ended up in the Samadhi Hall, and found the seat I'd hoped to occupy a few days earlier. The seat was directly across from my favorite smiling picture of Ramana. Soon after, a deep meditation and *samadhi* took over. I experienced a sense of the I-thought vanishing and attention being drawn deeper and deeper into the heart, until there was no difference between the perception of my experience and the Self I knew to be the Heart. All was One.

Mantra of this Dream

The next morning, I climbed the Mountain with Dai and his neighbor. We left early in the morning to try to beat the heat. As we climbed the 1,600 foot holy hill I felt extremely dizzy about halfway up, but then it passed. The *sadhus* at the top of the Mountain seemed to emit a stronger vibe of wanting a donation than last year. I left my donation under a rock by the large Shiva *lingam* instead. I had no doubt they would find it, it just felt right to give the offering to the Mountain directly.

I spent part of the afternoon meditating in my room before going to the Ramanasramam. Once in the Old Hall, a deep, and almost sleepy meditation overtook me. I was still tired from climbing the Mountain, but it felt different. It was a relaxation that was beyond my ability to define. It felt unique from the *samadhi* states I had been experiencing. There was no longer a sense of having a body, although I was still aware of watching any thoughts and the subtle arising of the I-thoughts in particular. Sometimes the thoughts had nothing to do with the experience of myself. It was as though I was profoundly empty and things were arising within the field of Consciousness.

Then, a series of chants began in the Samadhi Hall and continued into the Mother Shrine, echoing into the Old Hall. Some type of ceremony was in full progress, and soon the large hanging bell in the Mother Shrine began ringing. This ringing seemed to hollow out any thoughts that were lingering, as though I was empty and the vibrations were echoing inside me. The clang of the bell was everything. A woman's voice then sounded through the hall, softly chanting in a melodious tone. It was the first time I heard a woman leading a chant, since typically daily there are only Brahman priests and boys in attendance. Her voice carried the traditional tones and pitches of classical Indian music and her chanting was mesmerizing. When my body awareness returned, I felt chilled and incredibly expansive. A *samadhi* took over once more in a gentle wave, drawing me deeper into the meditative experience. I then fell into the vast space of the Heart.

My journal described this experience further: "It is all the mantra of the Heart, whether it is the Brahman priests chanting, the woman singing, visual scenes of colorful saris, men half dressed in traditional Indian clothing, the color of bright orange, devotees from different races, children's footsteps, parents scolding, a child laughing, a man coughing, a plume of incense lofting, the sounds and motions of bowing, Ramana's painted portrait, and the loud temple bell emptying my head, driving attention deeper into this great Source of the Heart. It was all the same."

Abundance

The next day, I returned to the Old Hall, but discovered that it was crowded. Luckily, there was one available seat right near Ramana's old couch. The waiting space even had a heavily padded cushion with good back support. I felt like a queen. After a long meditation session, I returned to the office to inquire about my cushion, for what I knew would be the last time. I wasn't sure anyone would remember me from our previous conversation because of the number of visitors, so I just began my story with saying, "I lost something." A clerk I had talked to briefly asked me to continue, so I explained about the small mat that I had lost in the Old Hall.

The clerk smiled and said that he remembered me, and since then had been looking for my mat. A kind, older man came out from the back office to witness our conversation, and stood smiling. The clerk explained that he discovered that a man had mistakenly used my cushion, but after talking to him the man gladly returned it. He left briefly to bring out what I thought would certainly be my little cushion.

To my surprise and near embarrassment, the man brought out a huge camping pad, ten times larger than the mat I lost. I held my heart and laughed in disbelief, and shook my head trying to explain that my cushion was small in comparison. I imagined the innocent man, who may have been riding the bliss of his meditation to suddenly be pressured by kindness to give up his camping pad. I hoped that they would find him to return it. All I could do was walk away with a full heart, smiling at God's sense of humor. The search for my cushion had ended.

A Moment's Blessing

I awoke the next morning smiling as I recalled a dream. I had been sitting in a large recliner in a narrow alley in India. I was watching all sorts of things pass by, but I remained in my chair, motionless. Dai appeared with his face painted like a *sadhu*. I greeted him saying that I knew he must have just returned from Ramana's lower cave. He agreed then continued on his way. Just then a flying black couch went past which looked like a cow. Again, I was just watching as everything was passing by. I stayed unmoving.

After leaving my room to check my e-mail, I noticed that a calf that died yesterday was gone from the Sadhu Trail. I guessed that the people who owned it must have decided to bury it. On my way back, it was again confirmed as I looked around the trail and could not find it. I returned to my room feeling better about the calf, relieved that the carcass was not just left there to rot and become scavenged by animals.

I learned that the calf belonged to neighbors of the internet business, and that they'd brought the mother cow to a veterinarian. The cow had been eating trash from a nearby field, likely the Sadhu Trail, and subsequently developed worms. The baby was also born with worms. I recalled seeing the calf early that morning nursing from its mother. It looked so wobbly and fragile, and cute. It was not until I learned the details of its death did I also remember seeing sadness in the owner's eyes, but thought I had been mistaken. Later that day, the calf died indicating that the owner likely knew it was ill but couldn't do anything to help.

I returned to my room to meditate. A few images kept arising, including the scene of the dead calf and also the girl with scabs on her back. These images, along with the disabled beggar near the temple would come and go throughout my meditation. I would continue to go deeper into the Source to recognize these images as coming from the mind. But the images returned. I would acknowledge them, but did not hold onto them nor dwell on them. I was reminded of how Shiva is both the destroyer and the creator of the Universe. All that is can be found in Shiva's endless cycles. The Source is where everything comes from and returns to. It didn't make sense in the mind, but something deeper seemed to completely understand this action. All was this movement of love, even death.

Later, I walked down the Sadhu Trail with plans to eventually end up at the Ramanasramam to complete my meditation. As I walked, the Mountain again seemed to pull at me. My heart felt the presence of the Mountain and the endless stream of love that seemed to emanate and fill me. I closed my eyes as I felt this blessing from the Mountain and the exchange of energy into my heart. When I opened my eyes a *sadhu* was about to pass by on the trail. He looked at me, holding his hands to his heart in prayer, saying, "Arunachala is God." I looked into his eyes ever so briefly but long enough to feel the connection of passing souls. At that the *Sadhu* said, "Thank You." It was a moment that seemed frozen in time. The exchange of energy was powerful and the sense of the Mountain included everything.

As I continued walking down the trail, I noticed something off to the side and immediately recognized it as the calf. It had been torn apart by the dogs and buzzards, and its intestines were lying nearby the remains of its body. Its cute face was still intact and untouched. There was a surreal sense that I was even seeing this, yet my heart was full and unmoving. It was like my dream. It was evidence of returning to the Source; all was a returning to the Source. All moments were a movement of Grace, even if my thinking mind could not understand or comprehend what was occurring. The calf nursing from its mother that morning, the mother's expression, the *sadhu* looking at me with recognition, the child crying, the dog nudging, my eyes witnessing, the Mountain in its Stillness, the dead calf now being eaten, feelings of compassion, all just a moment's blessing.

Nineteen

Deathless Spirit

Present moment awareness continues to reveal the nature of reality.
Our true essence, the Self, is here always.

The Guiding Heart

Returning to Ramana's lower cave to meditate, a deep meditation soon overtook me. Afterwards I became acutely aware that I have no clue about what is going to happen in the next moment. I can't be certain who I will meet during the day or if a relentless vendor might approach me, demanding I buy something. And, if I am asked, how will I respond? No matter how I feel in any moment, this does not mean I will feel the same five minutes from now. I noticed how the thoughts, feelings, sights, and sounds that arise have their own rhythm, and will arrive without me doing anything.

I was left understanding that all there is to do is show up in the sacred or present moment, openhearted without any expectations. Whatever is going to happen is in play and it has nothing to do with me. And, it never did and never will. So I tried this on, this simply showing up. This was my meditation and practice throughout the day.

My journal described my experience further, "I noticed immediately that the flavor of awareness deepened when I was in my heart. I noticed the bark on a passing tree, the butterflies and the dragonflies dancing in the wind, the rocks on the trail shaped like big hearts, and the warm breeze blowing my scarf. When I went back into my head, I observed thoughts of whether the elephant carver was angry because I hadn't purchased anything from him this year. Then back to the heart, I knew that whatever the vendor's reaction, if I decided to look at his carvings, or ended up walking away, it was simply the heart's action. It had nothing to do with me. There was a sense of joy and freedom with this realization, and I let the heart guide my next steps."

Who am I?

I returned to the Old Hall in the afternoon and allowed my mind to remain busy. I felt a gentle sense of directing attention back to the Source then witnessing all that was arising, especially paying attention to thoughts. Thoughts arose spontaneously, just as sounds or sights would arise. There was no difference. A sense of hollowness, a bodily emptiness took over. This started a series of self-inquiry questions of how I could even exist without the sense of a body. Who am I? What is this that exists beyond the body and in between the thoughts? Do thoughts define me? How can they if thoughts come and go? Do *I* come and go? I was inspired to visit Ramana's New Hall to read his account of his awakening, which was written in English. I knew that Ramana had a symbolic death experience when he was only sixteen. However, this was the first time visiting the wall-size account, and reading Ramana's description of his awakening in his own words.

I was drawn to a part of his account unfamiliar to me. It explained that, "Thoughts may come and go like passing notes but the sense of 'I' remained unchanging." This realization penetrated deep within me, as if it were my deepest knowing. I wrote later, "It was spoken so clear in Ramana's words. It truly does not matter if thoughts are arising or not. They do not supersede or surpass the primordial sense of 'I.' 'I' is changeless, all else will come and go. All sensations, all thoughts, including memories, experiences, and attachments will all recede like waves returning to the sea. The Sea of Consciousness, the Heart, remains the same."

Nothing Ever Happened

The next day as I was walking around the Mountain, the self-inquiry questions that had manifested the previous day continued, then deepened. My attention was directed into the Source of the Heart, since questions and answers were flooding in. I described this further in my journal: "Present moment awareness continually reveals the nature of reality. All is a manifestation out of this Source. It is all happening in the present moment. Nothing can be separate from this. Nothing was born and nothing dies. 'Where do I feel my father or my grandmother? Where do I feel my cat, Punky? Where is the sense of them even though they are dead?' The answers are all same. It is in this moment of presence that everything is experienced. There is nothing separate from this. It is all the Self in its different forms and manifestations, again only to be revealed in this precious moment."

That evening back in my room, I wrote the following, "It will be just four days until I will leave Tiruvannamalai. Yet, there is the sense of there being no time. It really doesn't matter where a person is. It is still the Self. The mind, with its creative manifestations, is just that. It is the Self that remains unchanging through everything. This is truly who I am."

The Deathless Spirit

I returned the next morning to the Ramanasramam. I was again drawn to read Ramana's account of his awakening. This time I focused on the description of how he knew himself to be the Deathless Spirit. He realized that the experiences of the body would come and go, breathing would come and go. When he held his breath, he knew that the presence of his own awareness, the 'I' was forever intact and unmoving. With his realization of being this Deathless Spirit, he continued his self-inquiry. "Who is this that experiences?" He knew himself as still intact with a personality even though he was not his body. I focused again on the words of how 'thoughts would come and go like passing notes, but the sense of 'I' was unchanging.' He wrote how he could engage in talking, reading, or other activities, but this sense of 'I' and his dwelling in this 'I' was permanent from that time forward.

Once in the Old Hall, I meditated on the Deathless Spirit, allowing energy to move through me, thoughts to pass, sounds to be heard. It was all a flow of divine energy, yet this was not my energy, nor my creation, nor my possession. It was Source, energy moving, experienced in this form, this body/mind, which came from the Source, and returned to the Source. The Mountain could be felt from within and without.

After my meditation, I walked to the entrance of the ashram. I intended to meet up with Dai and others who were planning to see a woman referred to as the Crazy Amma (Mother). She reportedly lived in caves and a tree for many years, including Papaji's Cave. She is known for giving powerful, spiritual transmissions. However, when it came time to leave by auto-rickshaw, I discovered that I wasn't motivated to accompany them. Instead, I returned to my room with the garlands I had purchased for Amma, knowing it would be a time of meditating in my room, a time to simply reside in the Heart.

Back in my room I recognized how my day had turned out differently than I had planned. I gazed at my altar, placing the garlands of fresh white and pink jasmine blossoms, and two roses (one from the Flower Sadhu) in front of Ramana's photo. The results were absolutely beautiful. I spent the next five hours meditating on the Source, which entailed repeatedly focusing my attention to rest in the heart space. When I would rest, I would be mindful of the heart. When I would meditate, sit, or eat, I would continue to be mindful of the heart space. I meditated on the Deathless Spirit and studied the mind's thought-patterns, observing how at times there was nearly constant motion. A thought may not be there, but I would sense an energy (subtle or obvious), while being aware of the mind trying to pull attention away from the Source. Mysteriously, even following this energy with alertness would eventually return to resting in the heart.

Before bed, I randomly chose a verse from *The Spiritual Heart— Bhagavan Ramana Answers* by A.R. Natarajan: "…The Self is the Heart. The world rises with the mind and sets with the mind. That which rises and sets is not the Self." These words penetrated my heart. I knew with certainty this is why spiritual experiences, words, and insights can never be the Self. They are always removed. Even the experience of the Self is still the one experiencing. I wrote, "It is to go beyond even this, to be one with the experience, not the experiencer of the experience!"

Eyes of Consciousness

Another vivid dream began my day. In this dream, I was jumping up then soaring into the air. When I became lucid, I remembered Joel's advice to touch something, then try to change something in the dream environment. I thought, "think pink" to change the color of the black stone ceiling I touched. The color of the ceiling did not change, but I fell backwards and was freefalling, no longer flying. Pink, fluffy clouds were below me. I arched my back and relaxed freefalling into the Heart of Awareness, a complete surrender. It was the same as going into the void during meditation, yet not startling out of this space. There was no fear, just falling deeper into the Self.

Late morning I went out walking, heading in the opposite direction. I spotted a small puppy with a large, open gash on his head. He was trying to rest but I could tell he was in pain. I saw an ambulance responding to someone ahead, an unusual sight for this area. A child was running out to the street urgently trying to get help for someone inside a house. I knew there would be no help for the puppy. I prayed to Shiva and continued to walk. I noticed how full yet neutral my heart felt. I could feel compassion, however I was not overwhelmed by what I was seeing and feeling. This too was God; this too was Consciousness. My eyes were the eyes of Consciousness and I knew it.

I thought about a dog I had witnessed having a seizure. I was upstairs looking out my back window, and could see the owner looking at the elderly dog. The dog staggered, struggling to keep on its feet, and finally leaned against a tree to remain upright. I watched the woman gazing at the dog, but she did not approach him. I realized she could not do anything to help the dog. I could see compassion in her eyes for the dog as she continued on with carrying water into her small house. I felt compassion and love for both of them.

I then came upon a mother dog scavenging through some garbage. I knew she must have puppies nearby by the size of her sagging teats. I called her to follow me to a nearby food stand, and bought several egg cakes for her. She was intelligent and patiently waited for me, then gently took my offering from my hands. I could tell she was ravenous, and the food did little to help fill in her skinny frame and protruding ribs. I felt pity for her hoping she would find more food as she trotted off searching.

The Monkey Sadhu

I continued to walk and decided to spend a few hours meditating in Ramana's lower cave. On the way to the main road, a *sadhu* started following me and was eager to talk to me. Steve had asked me earlier to try to film a *sadhu*, and interview him with my camera. We had filmed some monks we interviewed in Thailand, so I agreed if the opportunity availed itself in India I would do so. I ended up buying a cup of chai for the *sadhu,* in exchange for a little movie. It was an entertaining experience, as he acted like a monkey. In fact, I nicknamed him the Monkey Sadhu, and would sometimes admonish him, "Settle down Monkey." He was an unusually hyper *sadhu,* jabbering almost nonstop, or ranting, agitated. I recalled a recent dream where I was talking to a monkey, and guessed somehow it was a premonition of meeting him.

I wasn't planning on spending my last time on the Mountain in his company, but he became my shadow and seemed determined to walk the Mountain with me. It soon was apparent that the Monkey Sadhu was likely incapable of silence. If he wasn't talking to me, or ranting at someone who was passing by, he would talk to himself. At one point, he started blowing a conch shell he casually pulled out of his bag, bowed in front of me trying to kiss my feet, and even placed flower pedals where I would be stepping. He no doubt was mentally ill, but it was the Divine in just another disguise.

There wasn't much peace or quiet with him tagging along, however it was a wonderful opportunity to witness "monkey mind," or a busy mind in motion. I finally ditched the Monkey Sadhu near the Ashram, since it appeared he just might follow me back to my room.

But, he did provide some laughs. Later, I'd recall the times he would try to worship me, as if Consciousness was bestowing on me my first devotee. All my grand spiritual experiences and insights would earn me my first devotee: a mentally ill, wild *sadhu* who would sometimes run on all fours, flail his arms wildly if anyone would try to talk to me, and abruptly stop walking to pose in some unusual yoga positions. Again, it was so clear that the Universe has a sense of humor. Just in case I was becoming prideful of any spiritual obtainment, here was my reward.

Divine's Plan

As I walked back to my room, I spent some time standing on the Sadhu Trail gazing at the Mountain. I then noticed the same female dog I had given the egg cakes to earlier. She was tearing at the calf's carcass and I observed how I was now grateful that the owners had not buried the calf after all. I could see how everything had come full circle. I reflected on my judgmental mind and how I at first felt bad that the owner hadn't buried the calf. Yet now, I was happily witnessing this dog eating, knowing she was starving and had pups to feed. I could see how it was kindness for the family to leave the calf's body on the side of the Sadhu Trail. It was a gift, though my mind at first was certain that the correct action was to bury it. Now, it was being revealed there is a plan for everything, everyone, and every seemingly unrelated event. What an incredible blessing to witness this.

My journal concluded, "Even though my day turned out different than how I thought it might, I feel content and at peace. There is a divine plan, and I am just along for the ride."

Being With What Is

For my last day in India I was slow leaving my room. Combined with a budding respiratory illness and it being my last official day, I was surprised to notice a lack of heightened emotions associated with leaving. It felt quite different from last year's departure, yet my heart felt full. There wasn't time to walk one last time on the Mountain, but I'd realized this when the Monkey Sadhu invited himself on my walk the previous day. I spent the morning packing and reflecting on some of the highlights of the trip, and what spiritual lessons I would be bringing home from the Mountain.

"Being with what is" is one of the most important lessons I would bring home with me. For example, the simple act of not wearing earplugs while sleeping reflected this. During my first trip to India, I stayed in a noisy area of the village, so I would often sleep with earplugs, an eye shield, and a fan blowing loudly. Even with the earplugs, barking dogs would still occasionally wake me during the night, as would the traffic, the nighttime celebrations from distant temples, and the early morning Call to Prayer from the nearby mosque. However, for the most part I would sleep through most of the night. The second day into this trip, I stopped wearing the earplugs, feeling it was time to just be with whatever was arising. This meant if the dogs wanted to bark at 2:00 in the morning (which they invariably did), if there were firecrackers from a nearby ashram or some type of traffic or machinery, I would just allow myself to wake up, then be with what is.

I would then observe any reactions, whether negative or positive, whether I was making judgments, or just being curious. I learned to immediately accept and relax into whatever was arising, going into any resistance by bringing attention into the heart space. Everything was being experienced purely within myself. I was not separate from what was happening, even if I did not like it. There was no one to blame or be irritated at. It was all happening within me.

What started out as a subtle nighttime practice naturally evolved into how I went about my day. This meant accepting and not pushing away anything, including the heart-tugging sights of suffering, the filth, my own feelings of confusion, the bliss, the beggars grabbing at my clothes, the dead calf, the struggling, skinny ox being whipped, the disabled man who could only walk bent backwards, and so on. The opportunities to keep this practice of being with what is were endless.

If a beggar abruptly showed me their wounds, spit at me, or if I witnessed human or animal suffering, I would not look away. I would be fully present, emotionally and physically. Whatever I was feeling (anxiety, fear, sorrow, compassion, nausea, shock, or bliss), I would be with it, returning again and again to the space within that never changes. I'd focus on the heart of presence before sleep, and immediately upon waking, then would return to it throughout the day. Whatever was arising in life, the scenes I would see and sensations I would experience, I would be with what is. If someone was impatient and was pushing me from behind, I would be present to that. If words wanted to be spoken, I trusted that they would come. If they didn't, I accepted this as well.

The acceptance of what is seemed to build naturally. After awhile, I no longer needed to coach myself, or focus on bringing attention to the heart space. It would simply happen on its own. I started to notice a growing tolerance of being with discomfort, even my mind's discomfort. I didn't need to turn away from what was happening, on the outside or inside myself. Feeling contraction was a clue to be with whatever was happening, and fully bring awareness into the heart. Needless to say, in India there are plenty of opportunities for your edges to be smoothed (as my friend Dai would say). I could see this as true.

The Wisdom of the Heart

As I reflected on the journey into the heart, and the second trip to the sacred mountain Arunachala, I couldn't help but feel this was the true journey into the Heart Cave. Although the previous year's trip was bright with spectacular experiences and insights, and the retreats since had been brimming with heart openings, this trip seemed to show that the journey into the Heart never ends. I added to my journal, "Following the full surrender, experienced as a freefall into the heart space, it feels like another layer of deepening has occurred. The mind in its limitations can never understand the wisdom of the heart so will forever question and introduce doubt. This truth is something that cannot be understood or put into words. To surrender is to drop below the mind's understanding, or take a step back before the forming of thoughts, especially the I-thought. This is where the spacious nature of the limitless heart is revealed. There is no end to this mysterious unveiling of Consciousness. There is no end of this journey."

I walked the Sadhu Trail on my way to the Ramanasramam to bid farewell to the Old Hall, the Samadhi Hall, and the Mother Shrine. And, of course, I wanted to spend some time with my beloved Dancing Shiva statue, as well as a statue of Shiva and Shakti (Parvati) standing together. I had become more and more drawn to honor these two figures together. It seemed that the statues represented the name 'Shivananda,' the union of the Divine with the Manifest.

Walking in the front entrance of the ashram, I noticed the Saint, K.V.C., walking out of a side office. I stopped in the courtyard knowing somehow that he would pass my way. He walked in my direction, and recognized me. I told him of my departure. He said he had been gone for the past six days, and just returned back to the Ashram. The Saint asked me about this second journey to Tiruvannamalai, and asked if there would be a third. I answered that I thought I would no doubt return, and how each journey continues to deepen and deepen. He agreed, and said these simple words that felt very powerful, "The deeper you go, and soon you only live by the words of Bhagavan." I thanked him and we both offered a Namaste greeting as we left. I felt that indeed this was one more blessing, and felt my heart centered in love.

My last greetings to each of the statues in the Mother Shrine, and visiting the Old Hall and his Samadhi Hall were also sweet. Yet, I was not overcome with bliss or anything extreme. There was just a knowing comfort that all was in divine order. I left the Mother

Shrine feeling Shiva's smile, and then felt a strong urge to stand near the statue of Shiva once more.

I ended my pilgrimage in the New Hall, reading Ramana's description of his awakening, in particular his death experience. I focused on how he knew he was not the body, and how the sense of 'I' was beyond the body. In his final months his cancer had metastasized, and it was obvious to others that he was in extreme pain. Yet, this did not stop him from residing in the experience of the Self. He was the Self, not the body, and that is how he lived. I thought about my illness being an opportunity to experience the Self, the "Deathless Spirit," which is beyond the cold symptoms my body may be feeling.

I met Dai one last time at our regular chai stand. He would be staying on for a few more months. I hadn't pulled out my camera all day believing that I was through snapping photos and had captured enough, and seen enough. Then suddenly, there came the cacophony of horns blasting, cymbals crashing, drums beating, and people dancing and chanting. A funeral procession was coming down the street, toward us, then stopped right in front of us. At that moment, I spotted a young *sadhu* with bright orange canvas high tops, and starting snapping photos. Consciousness was again showing its many colorful manifestations. It was my send off, another unexpected blessing.

However, when it came to my taxi ride, this seemed to be a different matter. With all the stops for trains, and the driver wanting to buy snacks and drinks on more than one occasion, I was nearly late for my flight out of Chennai. However, as is frequently the case, everything works out in mysterious ways. This time, it allowed me to have a quiet airport check-in, and I actually lost my assigned seat, yet a better one became available. I even had a little time to gaze at the Shiva statue located in the airport.

Traveling Mindfully

Surprisingly, returning home was one of the most poignant times of my trip. Despite going without sleep for nearly forty-eight hours, there was just presence. Whether meditating on the plane, listening to music by Enya, or just being, I was so aware of not being the doer. I wrote, "It is all this play of Consciousness and still mysteriously, nothing is really happening. Nothing is happening because there is literally only stillness, but in the manifestation of being human, there is the illusion of motion, activity, mind, and life. *Om*. It is true. We are all this Deathless Spirit. I was reminded of the Saint's words, 'The deeper you go, and soon you only live by the words of Bhagavan.' I could feel the truth of those words, feeling tears of gratitude as I dipped again and again into the radiance of my own heart, then rested there."

PART VII:

Finding the Teacher Within

Twenty

Mountain Resting?

*"When the search has stopped itself there is a deep knowing
of One mind."*
~Marlies Cocheret[27]

Coming Out

Two weeks following my return from India, my reentry back to home and work continued to feel seamless. "Being with what is" had become my life motto. I wrote, "By living in acceptance of whatever is happening in the present moment there is the continual invitation to just be. Relaxing into any areas of contraction naturally returns to a space of expansion. My heart continues to feel full and at peace."

Over the next month, several changes were starting to happen in my life. At work, I chose to transfer from my assignment even though it had offered a nice office, predictability, and security. I felt the need to be freer in my life and heart. However, changing my assignment proved only to be the beginning. Something internal was pushing me to create more space, to not be pinned down. At first I wasn't sure for what, but soon the heightened creativity to write spiritual and personal growth books was ever present. Before long, I would have three writing projects going. I then felt a burning impulse to resign my full-time position at the hospital.

The Mystery had taken over and I knew it. I had never trusted anything more in my life. The presence within was everything. My mind would occasionally stir, tossing out worries about living in poverty, and the craziness of giving up my career for something that wasn't tangible. However, the power over this movement was a kin to giving birth. The energy felt urgent, like a need to give myself life. I could no longer deny who I really was. I was coming out of the spiritual closet.

Steve questioned my decision, and voiced concerns that we would not have enough income to make it. However, I believed with certainty that something would work out, even if it were to stay on at the hospital in a relief position. I felt guided.

In March I gave notice at my job, and a few days later met Marlies Cocheret, another awakened teacher. Marlies is a student of Adyashanti and lives in Santa Cruz. It was nearly two months since I'd returned from India. Her flyer had a quote that caught my attention: "When the search has stopped itself there is a deep knowing of One mind." Somehow, I knew I was supposed to meet her and would be mysteriously facing a reflection of myself. I hoped to meet her privately as there was a question I wanted to ask her. However, there would be no time for a private session due to both of our schedules.

Her public *satsang* was being offered at a private home in Eugene. I felt drawn to sit directly in front of where she would be sitting. I sat looking at this beautiful woman with eyes of compassion, and felt she was in touch with the bliss of the Divine. After her monologue, the floor was open for questions. I raised my hand and began with the first question, which was no longer customary for me.

The words poured out: "I have been living my spiritual path to the point I can no longer stay in the spiritual closet. My life is currently like a crumbing tower. It is time to fully live congruently and not hide this aspect of myself any longer. I have been one to experience many heightened spiritual experiences. Any one of them you would think was enough to lead to enlightenment. However, in the end, I have discovered that these spiritual experiences mean very little. The space within that never changes is what I always return to, no matter what this mind or body wants to do. I used to have the experience of the heart, which was greatly limited to the physical realm with occasional floodings of there being no boundaries. Now, the shift has happened where there are no boundaries between inside and outside. There is no separate one from what is experienced. It is all the Divine. Yet, with this knowing I have never received confirmation from any of my teachers. I in no way want to delude myself or anyone else. Yet, there is this great pull to share with others, and not hide this knowing any longer. It is what I am, and my life is becoming a reflection of that. I know I am not separate from this unfolding."

Marlies looked at me with her knowing eyes and said these simple words, "Only you can know that you have gone far enough. Nobody can ever tell you that or confirm your own knowing. You are the one that knows. If you feel you have gone far enough, then you have." My heart knew clearly. I knew I had gone far enough in my seeking, and I also knew this journey never ends. I felt love rushing in with the acknowledgment of this truth. I knew Grace is what would continue to carry me in this life. I was already home.

Twenty-One

Devotion and the End
of Separation

Any sense of self that comes and goes cannot be the Self.

For the next six months a deepening and resting in my true nature continued. My mind had periods of calmness in which I was free from any doubt. I never asked Joel for validation, nor told anyone at the Center about the awakening. Yet, like before, this was not enough for a mind like mine with such powerful conditioning to know and understand. All I had been shown, in the end, once again, was not quite enough. The quality of awareness and the discovery of the space within that never changes was still with me. However, the mind with its steady and relentless movements was again pulling me back into the world of delusion. Even though I could observe the thoughts arising, I found it difficult to recognize these thoughts as truly being Consciousness and not the workings of my individual identity.

In October, I wrote the following: "Again, it seems impossible that with so many tastes of the Divine, with Consciousness revealing itself daily, that I would still listen to my mind. I even know better! But still, I do it. It was subtle at first, and then before long I found myself believing what my mind would feed me. The meeting with Marlies satisfied my seeking for about six months. Her quote still resonates within me, and I can sense deeply the truth of her words: 'When the Search has stopped itself there is a deep knowing of One Mind.' I certainly know this to be true. My God, how many times have I seen this, yet it is not enough. Here I am seeking to go on yet another spiritual retreat. Seeking apparently is not done in my life. The mind has crept in, and questions the sense of presence and peace I have had since returning from India. Why do I even listen?"

So, on October 13th I returned to Cloud Mountain to attend another 10-day retreat with Joel, the topic being the path of Bhakti and Jnana, or devotion versus the quest for truth. As I began the retreat, I wrote a journal entry that summarizes some of my activities before the retreat.

"As I start this retreat let me catch up by saying that I am still working a lot at the hospital, although in a relief position. I offered some Radiant Heart mini-retreats and personal growth seminars at our home and at two healing centers in Eugene, as well as one in Minnesota while visiting my sisters. I also continue to write. I no longer see David; the last time was at a brief public *satsang* this summer. I have been attending the Center regularly and meditating about 45 minutes daily, and just living my spiritual path by keeping my heart open to life. So here I am at another retreat. We will see what happens."

Joel began the retreat by explaining the differences between the two spiritual paths (or yoga paths) of Bhakti and Jnana. Bhakti Yoga requires an invitation to have a union with the Divine, God. For the Bhakta, the path leads to a full surrender to the object of devotion. Motivation on the spiritual journey is driven by an intense longing to experience the Divine, or to know God. The separate self is eventually destroyed through this union of love, like an insect being attracted to a flame. Jnana Yoga is the path of knowledge, and the Jnani is driven deeper on the spiritual journey by their sincere desire to know the Truth, no matter what they may find. The Jnani experiences a burning curiosity to know the truth about God, about who they are, and the meaning of life.

We were reminded how both paths converge at the end, and how the practice of self-inquiry helps us gain insights about what is true. By seeking beyond our intellectual understanding, we are able to gain experiential insights, a necessary step in gaining a naked or pure experience. Joel told us that it is important to understand that the physical sensations we believe ourselves to be are only the breath and bodily awareness. There is no separate self other than the One, only a sensed perception of individual form. Our imaginations are what cause suffering.

Over the course of the retreat, Joel taught variations of the Choiceless Awareness meditation so we could observe the impermanence of thoughts, emotions, and even self-identity (our personal stories).

Choiceless Awareness Meditation (Observing Thoughts) taught by Joel Morwood

1. Drop labeling. During the choiceless awareness meditation, your attention gently observes what is arising in the sensory fields. Drop labeling what you are experiencing. The goal is to simply experience the "suchness" of phenomena arising.

2. Allow thoughts to arise, then allow them to self-liberate. The goal is not to push away thoughts or become judgmental about them. Thought is not your enemy; instead don't feed the story.

3. Surrender even subtle efforts to keep attention still. Attention will have the sense it is fluid, which it is. However, it contains serenity. It is the ocean or sky. There is stillness ultimately, even though the waves or clouds of thoughts will pass.

4. Just let things come and go. By not getting lost in effort, or your conditioned state, there is simply relaxed choiceless awareness; this is your natural state.

**Choiceless Awareness (Relaxed Version),
taught by Joel Morwood**

1. First establish clarity and stability by following the breath or concentration object.

2. Enter Spacious Awareness.

3. Without grasping or pushing away, look directly at thoughts. Watch the story arise, without getting sucked into it.

Joel explained how our self-identify, the "Story of I," maintained by pursuing worldly happiness eventually loses its importance. Often this is replaced by a spiritual story, yet there is still an individual 'I.' The story then becomes the spiritual quest. Joel said it is a necessary step on the spiritual path, but this path too will eventually end. It is the mind that continues to follow us into our inner life. This is why the study of impermanence is so important. By understanding how all things come and go, we also observe our spiritual story. Does the story come and go?

During a meditation, I watched as the story that made up my life began to disappear. My journal describes this: "I don't exist. I am already dead. What is the purpose of all of this? Everything I strive for, set goals for, will end. It is all impermanent. The ultimate test is my devotion and commitment for Ramana and Shiva. It is only Consciousness. The inner stillness is the only aspect and taste I have of what is eternal. All else is at death's doorstep."

Next, Joel sent us out on an assignment. We were to go and find an independent, existing object and bring it back in the evening. I wrote after coming back empty-handed, "Nothing exists without the experiencer. Outside and inside are experienced as One. It is all a total and pure experience of Consciousness. It is like a diamond of pure radiant light. Each facet is reflecting an image or window of itself, as well as back to itself. Devotion is the guiding light to point the direction of the one abiding Truth. It is the only thing that is permanent and beyond the perceived limits of time, death, and worldly existence. Yet, in emptiness there are no forms, it takes this relationship of forms for devotion to occur."

As the retreat progressed, Joel guided us deeper, exploring the truth of ourselves and what boundaries actually exist. For me, this would lead to a standoff with my beloved objects of devotion, Ramana and Shiva, and my mind entering into a tailspin. At one point, I even contemplated going home. I did not want to hear any more.

Reluctantly, I returned for another session. Joel led a guided meditation in which we were to recall a time of anger, then a time of joy. My journal describes my experience: "The anger was so intense, my brain felt electric, just buzzing with energy. When the joy experience came to mind, I chose when I was one with Arunachala. I brought up a vivid image of bliss, was overcome with spaciousness and dipping into a *samadhi*. Joel then instructed us to let it go. I saw it nearly completely self-liberate, enough to show my held belief of how I viewed myself as a spiritual being. Did this come and go? What appears and disappears cannot be who we are. I could see that I had been holding onto the emotions and identity of what it meant to be a devotee of Ramana, and the feelings of being at the sacred mountain Arunachala."

Joel then sent us off for a solo day with Choiceless Awareness instructions on how to work with emotions.

Choiceless Awareness (Working with Emotions)
by Joel Morwood

1. Give the mind more free rein. Set the intention to remain aware (lucid) in the midst of whatever story arises.

2. To benefit from the story, keep the energy and clarity, then inquire into what is coming up.

3. Ask yourself, "What is left of me when the emotions are gone, self-liberate?" Watch how the emotion exists, then disappears. Allow the emotion to linger long enough to gain insight into the story.

4. Take apart the story with an inquisitive mind and do not reject what you learn.

5. Experience is your teacher. Discover what hooks you, then if this is who you really are.

Important to the instructions is to watch how the emotion exists, then disappears, allowing the emotion to linger long enough to obtain insight into the story. Joel said, "How else are we going to find out what is really going on?"

Already feeling conflicted and confused about what was arising earlier, it did not take long to generate an emotional story. I wrote, "I am tired of this spiritual game that ebbs and flows, the experiences, the insights that come and go. What is it all for, or leading to, that I haven't already glimpsed? The truth of who I am is not fleeting and does not change. My identity as a spiritual seeker, the one who strives for landmarks (a clear sign that this is awakening) is the one I am sickened by. This is not a game that will be won, and there is no concrete success to be held up like a trophy. Is this me? The story is just that, and will ramble on and on. Still, I remain solid and unchanging. And, what about the story of my love of the Divine?"

I left Joel another note asking how does one untangle the spiritual story versus the relationship with the Divine?

The evening lesson was about the three common pitfalls that spiritual seekers can fall into: 1). Misunderstanding the significance of emotions arising, 2). Mistaking experiences for enlightenment; since anything that comes and goes isn't what we are looking for, and 3). Mistaking thoughts for direct insights into enlightenment itself. The antidote for each was to watch mindfully, and allow these habits to fade on their own, or self-liberate. Joel reminded us that listening to our thoughts was not where experiential insights are found. What remains under all the phenomena arising and falling away is what we are looking for. The experiencer, or witness, is still there when everything vanishes. Who is that one?

The Show Down

The next morning, we were told that really there is no one to be enlightened, and no one to be deluded. When we start believing that enlightenment means finding a true thought, this is the mind's game at work. Thoughts are not true, and not false either. A thought is merely a thought. Thoughts try to seduce us, so the goal of the practice is to not get sucked in. Joel said it is like thoughts whisper, "Listen to me, I am the true thought." (Boy, do I know this one!) Brahman, the unchanging and infinite, is out of reach of thought. The mind can never understand our true essence. The mind will never get it.

Joel answered my question about differences between the spiritual story and the relationship with the Divine. All stories are based on distinctions. Thus the Divine, our relationship to it, is all imaginary. It is the form of the Divine. The relationship with the Divine is a boundary and must be eliminated. It is still a thought. He used the analogy of devotion being the ladder to reach the Divine, to Consciousness, but explained that we need to leave behind the ladder when we no longer need it. To reach union with God the seeker must tread along the path of unknowing. It leads beyond the spiritual story, beyond experiences and thoughts.

I woke in the morning remembering an odd dream: A tent containing my belongings was on fire. Steve and another person from the retreat were tending it. Joel was teaching in the next room, which was divided by a red curtain.

In the morning, another participant rose to get something in the dining room. For a moment, I thought I was the one getting up. I was so surprised that I was not also walking. It felt like the boundaries of self and other were slipping. It seemed almost that I was dreaming, but I wasn't.

Joel continued his teachings. The final crisis for the Bhakta is giving up that final separation between the sense of self and the image of the Divine. The truth of these words stung my heart.

In the afternoon, I wrote to my objects of devotion: "Dear Ramana, Can I see you beyond name and form? This love I hold for you, this guiding light I contribute to you, can I be the experiencer of the light itself? The beauty of your eyes, can I see they are but my own? To let go of the devotion and love I feel seems like a sin. To turn my back on you seems I am walking away from Truth. The sacred mountain Arunachala is a named image, not in sight, only held in the creation of my mind. You are not here in form, but I feel what I believe is your presence in my heart. Shiva, my lover, you too I must walk away from. Again, naming and separating from the Divine is only a play of the mind. But, what of this aching heart to even imagine this separation? I have delayed this day for as long as I have been able. Your mantras that flow in beauty are seen as words dividing. The division, the boundary must be destroyed. The fire must burn to complete and total union, until no one, no separate one is left standing."

To Kill the Buddha

Later in the evening, my journal continues: "All of this is happening without me doing or deciding anything. It is all this play unfolding, parallel paths sometimes colliding, order and rhythm in the seeming chaos of it all. And…back to the eyes of Ramana. Do I dismantle my altar? I don't want this story of my love for Ramana and Shiva, my felt connection to end. God forgive me, I must cut off the head of the Buddha, and shatter the statue. Now this takes a total and complete trust in the teachings of the Mystics. It goes against my heart to not utter the mantras I have come to adore, to not stare like a starry-eyed lover into Ramana's eyes, to not imagine my Shiva close by. It is time. I shall dismantle my altar, put all pictures and reminders of the Divine out of sight, and not say my beloved mantra for Ramana. Oh God, here I go… It's done. Is the mantra '*Om*' acceptable? Oh the mind trying to save anything from a devotional practice that it can."

Next Joel talked about the need to exhaust the inquiry in order to awaken. For a Jnani, it is said the average self-inquiry path takes approximately ten to twenty years, but, of course, it can be shorter or longer. For the Bhakta, the path is typically much faster, at least in the initial and middle stages. However, the end becomes the hindrance because of the love for the object of devotion. It is also possible to combine the two paths as I have done. For both the Jnani and Bhakta, each practice leads back to the Source. For the Jnani, the practice is to follow a thought to the end, or a sound to stillness. Attention needs to ride the phenomenon to its ending. For the Bhakta, he or she can follow the *Om*, the sound of Brahman, or another mantra to its end. This also takes us right back to the Source, since both paths converge, leading towards the end of seeking.

As I watched the clouds pass overhead in a clear blue sky, it was like ocean waves in a calm sea. My journal continued, "Everything, including all aspects of myself, is seen to be arising and passing away. Any sense of self that comes and goes cannot be the Self. Wow. It is so true. All of life, the silence, the stillness, all unseen and unmanifested, contains absolute potentiality. With my eyes gazing at the sky, I nearly ran into Joel on the path. It was the divine dance."

Feeling more centered, I returned for the afternoon session. The Radiant Heart, Consciousness itself, the ground of being was described as being a wordless experience. If we follow attention to the Source, it must be followed completely to the end without a trace. Joel talked about how following a big juicy thought, one with a lot of energy, creates a big hole. We continue to follow what is arising to its complete end, to emptiness. This emptiness includes everything. (This practice reminded me of many of the practices I was undertaking in India, like catching the tail of the I-thought, falling into the pinhole, or even following contraction into expansion.) A few more instructions were added, including that after following thoughts to their source, and when the thought is gone without a trace, we then need to surrender effort. If we don't, it can confuse the mind. Once you touch the ground (the Source), it is time to stop. Joel talked about kenosis, the Greek word for emptiness, which is when everything comes to a stop. We can't bring about kenosis by free will, but exhaustion or absolute contentment can. He explained that this space is different than calm abiding. Kenosis comes before Gnosis, or spiritual truth, since clarity, or a mind that's been emptied is needed for Truth to be known. For Gnosis, it requires a seeker to realize that there is no self, and "I am Consciousness itself." He reminded us that if a seeker realizes only one aspect of the Truth, then there is only one eye open, or only one shoe has dropped.

Here is my journal entry: "I put back my altar. I knew with certainty the divine objects and any acts of devotion were still Consciousness, just a different face or facet of the Truth. By turning away from this, it is pushing away an aspect of myself. It is still all Buddha, the object and subject. To turn away, paradoxically, creates even more duality. I knew the Buddha, the Divine, and I to be one, and always had been. I left Joel a note: 'Killed the Buddha.'"

Twenty-Two

Exhausting the Search

Once the search is exhausted, Truth can be found.

When to Stop

J oel talked about the self, explaining imagination is what keeps the self going. Our life is like a movie with the continuity of characters. However, a movie requires separate film frames to create the storyline. The many frames that piece together the movie are playing so fast that viewers don't notice the spaces in between, the gaps. Our lives unfold in the same way. It is to see when the self is there and when it isn't. Where are the gaps? I believed that was important to his teaching, since the goal was not to permanently get rid of the boundary of self and other. Instead, it is to identify this boundary as an illusion so we are no longer deluded. In fact, he suggested that we stop trying to get rid of anything. Delusion is the only thing we are trying to see through, which unravels the whole "Story of I."

He continued by talking about his teacher, Dr. Franklin Merrell-Wolff.[28] Dr. Wolff reportedly was never able to silence his thoughts, even after his own awakening. His strategy was to look at the sense of self, then look out from that space. Specifically, by looking inward, he taught his students to visualize a pole where the light of Consciousness emanates from. By practicing detaching from arising phenomenon, the focus then turns to the source of attention (the Heart). Joel commented that it is to find out where the looking is coming from. (I thought how this has been my practice for over two years.) Joel then read a quote by Ramana Maharshi: "If the mind is turned inward, objective knowledge ceases and the mind resides in the heart as the Self."

Seeing through the Game

After lunch, I walked on the path near the meditation hall. I was looking at the sunbeams glistening through the trees and listening to the birds. I was struck by an overwhelming temptation to laugh. I realized that my search was looking for something that could only be found in the one Consciousness, in which all is a part of. It dawned on me that I have looked for form in emptiness, and emptiness in form, but did not realize until that moment they are one and the same. I cannot experience or be one without the other—always. I laughed thinking how I was looking for a who in a what, and a what is a who, like it was still two separate things, two separate instructions. 'I,' the Self, Consciousness just is. The words themselves had formed a distinction in my mind, which I suddenly saw through.

Joel's final teachings were a review and added a few key points on what constitutes enlightenment. As the paths of the Jnani and Bhakta converge, we reach the end of spiritual seeking. "Not even God or Guru can help you at this point." He told us if we meet the Buddha on the road to kill him, but not in the beginning of our practice. All teachings are stage specific. He explained that the individual seeker can never become enlightened, because neither a true nor deluded self exists. Joel told us that there is no missing piece to enlightenment. It is here! It is only the mind that looks for the missing piece for its own understanding. Our effort to find enlightenment is a moving away from what is here now. He told us if we are looking for something, it is duality. The seeking for enlightenment is what distracts us from enlightenment. All of our practices launch us 99.999 percent on our path, but then seeking becomes the obstacle. This is when doing nothing becomes important.

With the retreat ending, I met with Joel. This was the first time I talked with him privately since returning from India. I described some of my experiences, the unchanging presence within me, and how the perception of outside and inside was now perceived as the same. His response? A story of a monk he has told me at least three times. The story goes something like this: A monk goes to his master telling him of his experience of awakening. The master says no that isn't it, and instructs the monk to keep looking. The monk, feeling perplexed goes away, but returns the next day. He tells the master that the master can keep *his* enlightenment and he will keep his. He told me that seeking is a call from wisdom. To not continue to seek when the path has not ended is turning away from the truth. Total and complete honesty is called for. Only I will know when I have reached understanding. I explained that my conditioning was strong, and I wanted to be certain I was being completely honest regarding my path and sense of awakening.

After meeting with Joel, I wrote the following, "Despite his words, him questioning my understanding, and my doubts, I still feel absolutely positive in my heart. Joel said that I should watch for the mind's stories of self, grasping, self-centeredness, and suffering. I will know the path has not ended if there are separate stories of formed identity, or the spiritual stories. He said there would be an undeniable certainty that what is experienced is Reality. The mind will then be satisfied and put to rest. This does not mean that the mind will not have continued thoughts, and occasional stories about certain things, there just will not be the sense of a self attached. Joel gave me the final words, 'don't be afraid of don't know mind,' something he has told me many times before. So, this retreat ends with me finding greater clarity that the truth can only be found within me. It is to rest in That."

Back in the Fire

Over the next six months, I was writing less often in my journal. A sense of simply being was taking over my life. However, in April 2007, I wrote, "I believe I am going through some dark night of the soul. I am taking a break from writing, and somehow have been feeling directionless and goalless. I cannot, or currently am not, visualizing anything concrete as far as having a plan, nor the will to see it through. I care and don't care. It is what it is. I can have all the hopes and dreams, yet it means little. Life has meaning, yet it is without meaning. Even striving for more spiritual understanding leads nowhere. There is nothing to hold onto. I have been in this space before. This is nothing new. I guess if there was something new, I don't even care. It is what it is, until it changes and isn't anymore. Then, it is what it is, all over again. I guess it is a good state to be in by Joel's standards."

Seeing Through the Sacred Cow

I was back at Cloud Mountain for another retreat in late April, the five-day Spring Retreat. I wrote, "My mental state inspired me or de-spired me to go it alone getting up here. It is not like I was without options. It wasn't always easy driving, with getting lost a few times, having sore legs, and being tired. But, I have no regrets. I wanted the quiet time, alone time. There is not much to say, I am here, even though I have been and continue to feel ambivalent about seeing this through. This is one of the reasons I drove up alone, in case I wanted to leave early, something I have never done before. I have one of my favorite rooms, but other than that, I did not bring an altar, am performing different chores, and just trying to be present to what is. There are no great feelings or hope that anything will change regarding spiritual insights, enlightenment. What can change? This space is what is, and never changes."

The retreat was co-facilitated by Fred Chambers and Joel. The title sparked my interest, since it was called The Unmovable Mountain. We were to stay accepting and unmoving to what is.

Throughout the retreat and choiceless awareness meditations, we were to return to being a mountain.

Fred and Joel took turns teaching and instructing us on our meditation practices. There were some unique instructions, but for the most part, the teachings were things I'd heard before. I was listening for gems of wisdom, and didn't take many notes, which was unusual for me. I found myself observing myself, as I listened to the instructions, feeling surprised that I was even at the retreat. Why had I chosen to be here? I assumed that my ambivalence would pass as the retreat progressed, but surprisingly, it didn't. I then told myself to just look at the time away as a vacation from work, and use the time to relax. So I was just showing up, but did not have any expectations. I was tired of having expectations.

Joel talked about enlightenment, which made my ears perk up a little. He mentioned that enlightenment is that which cannot be doubted, and insight is without content. Fred talked about relaxing in the heart area, and sinking down into this space. He told us to relax there. As thoughts arise, being in this space then helps us to not get lost in them. Fred instructed us to look over the shoulder of thoughts, into the cloud of unknowing, and for us to pay attention to the space it arises out of. Fred said we treat our thoughts like sacred cows. I smiled as I thought of India. We follow them and bow to them. Instead, remove your attention from them and let them wander away. In doing this we are able to taste freedom.

The Enso

During the teachings my attention continually focused on the large hanging tapestry of an Enso, a Zen Buddhist symbol of enlightenment. An Enso is generally drawn as a single thick brush stroke creating one full circle, however there is a slight break or gap where the brush stroke begins and ends. Many times I have sat in the hall meditating or listening, but this time I felt that the symbol was teaching me. I simply observed that something was being revealed on a mysteriously deep level, a place where the mind could not forage. I came up with these realizations: First, out of nothing, everything arises, then returns to nothing. Second, the breath is the beginning, but not just a beginning practice, and leads to the end of the path to enlightenment. And, third, by following the Enso it reveals the whole of Reality.

After the group session, I returned to sit alone in the meditation hall, gazing at the Enso. I realized that the end of seeking was somehow linked with this symbol, as if there was a message contained within it. The insights about the Enso then seemed to flood in. Each time we glimpse the Truth, we move into the open closure of the Enso, which is the gap. This is where presence, or the spaciousness of who we are is revealed. It is our own awareness—quiet, still, alive, and spacious without boundaries. The gap is the space within that does not change, and is the Heart of Awareness. The more we attune to the space, the gap, the greater our perception of this space grows. It is then possible to recognize what is here all the time.

I recognized the Enso as the whole spiritual journey. It was revealing the dance of impermanence in motion. All seeking arises out of the gap. Do we begin again, following the circle in search for enlightenment, or do we realize the whole spiritual search is a manifestation of Consciousness? I could see the whole ego-ridden story of self and arising phenomena (our thoughts, perceived struggles, and experiences) were also included in the Enso. The

Enso is taking place on the screen of our own awareness, which is Consciousness. I knew I was making the search too complicated, still looking for something greater than myself, beyond the sense of an individual 'I.' I had failed to see that even seeking was arising out of the gap, and the search was simply returning to the gap.

No one to be Enlightened

The retreat continued with Joel giving us a final teaching about enlightenment, saying it can never be found in our thoughts. And, paradoxically, it is not something *we* can ever find. This is because there is no one to be deluded, and no one to be enlightened. I could sense the Truth of his words. Enlightenment does not happen to a separate one. We only need to see through the veil of delusion (separation), so we can recognize what is here all the time. But, even this recognition, is an act of Grace.

The retreat was coming to an end. The last day would be solo practice and a time to meet with the teachers privately.

Once again, I went to talk to Joel. Same scenario: I described my ever-deepening process, yet still returning to the core sense of solidity I know to be the Truth or Consciousness. Despite whatever mind states I experience, this is where I return. Joel acknowledged deepening, yet pointed out that I was still seeking enlightenment that only exists in the mind. He said if I had discovered Truth I would be absolutely stopped in any further need for confirmation. If there is still one that seeks, it is to find that one. If there is still that one, there is not realization. I explained my quandary and hesitation regarding what to do with what I know. Joel responded if any such questions are arising then it is not realization. I explained that in my own life there was a growing comfort in unknowing, and that nobody in the outside world cares whether I am realized or not. But, because of my affiliation with the Center, I feel inclined to share what is happening. No further response from Joel. He had given his answer. Once the search is exhausted, Truth can be found.

I ended the retreat with the following journal entry: "I trust this knowing, it is all there is. Regarding me having an identity, I exist in the sense of there being a conceptual make-up, thoughts, and emotional conditioning. But, they are just that. This, too, is Consciousness."

The next morning I was up early. I completed my chores, and left the retreat before final check-in. I just didn't feel like there was anything more to say, do, or attain. I felt tired of the spiritual chase, the game of student and teacher, and seeking validation for something that nobody can own, or even really speak about anyway. I just felt done.

Twenty-Three

From Seeker to Finder

The Spiritual Finder has discovered the truth of who they are, and found Consciousness to be something that is and can only be forever present, before seeking and afterwards, in any and all circumstances.

Beyond Teacher

A bout a month following the retreat with Joel, I attended a *satsang* given by Tom Kurzka. The group turned out to be small that day so I felt obliged to take a turn sitting up with him. I didn't have a question to ask so we just sat in heartfelt silence, looking into each other's eyes.

Tom eventually broke the silence, saying that he had just returned from a retreat given by David and believed it was important for my spiritual development for me to go see him. I was shocked. I reminded him that I had worked with David in the past, and that this was no longer the path for me. Tom persisted, saying that few teachers on the West Coast could help me move beyond the prolonged state of kenosis (emptiness) I have been in, and help me complete the deep emotional work needed to break free.

I explained that I was not seeking another teacher to give me something. There was unease in not taking his advice, but I believed I needed to trust my own intuition. I told Tom that if this was all to my experience of Consciousness, I was okay with it, adding I would trust that deepening would happen in its own time. Tom's final advice was for me to deeply look at and experience emotions thoroughly, letting them burn the final layers of ego protection and resistance. Only then would I reach Gnosis, enlightenment.

When I returned home I thought about Tom's feedback, replaying his advice over and over in my head. I walked near a wooded stream to clear my mind. As I attuned to the presence, feeling my breath fill the spaciousness of my heart space, I listened to a spiritual talk on my iPod, given by John Sherman.[29] His teachings spoke to my heart, reverberating a truth I knew deep down. I did not need to go anywhere or do anything. An understanding came to me. Awakening is to simply be who we are, without trying to change anything.

A few weeks later, I scheduled a meeting with Todd Corbett from the Center. His eventual awakening was based on emotional work, primarily grief. We met five days before Steve and I were to leave for a vacation to Bali, Indonesia. Todd confirmed that there is no teacher that could give me what I needed besides simply focusing on the inner work and feeling emotions thoroughly. He suggested that I didn't need to worry about a deeper level of awakening, saying it will happen on its own. He explained that according to the Dzogchen Teachings, a teacher would likely tell me, "You have recognized the Mind, now continue practicing for the next 30 years." He advised me to not let the mind interpret and look for the end goal, instead to simply hold space for the endless possibility.

Ripe for Awakening

It has been said that awakening is like a mango dropping from the tree at the perfect time. All the teachings, feedback, and journeys into the Heart had propelled me this far, now it was time for Grace to complete the rest. There wasn't anything more 'I,' as a separate one seeking could accomplish.

I arrived in Bali with Steve in mid-June, 2007. The densely-populated island is 93 percent Hindu, while the surrounding Indonesian Islands are 85 percent Muslim. Our stay coincided with the holy Hindu festivals of Galungan and Kuningan. Galungan is a tribute to the defeat of good over evil, while Kuningan celebrates ancestral spirits. Each is ten days long. The cities and villages we visited were adorned with tall bamboo poles woven decoratively with young coconut leaves. Women carrying flat baskets on their heads with flowers and food offerings were a common sight, as were the lavish weddings, intimate family feasts, lively parades with dancing barongs (lion-dog figures), and elaborate funeral processions. It seemed that everywhere devotional practices were taking place throughout the day. Both women and men would decorate their family temples, after which the women would walk to their neighborhood temples to offer flowers and food. Even the photo of Ramana I had set on a small table found fresh flowers around it each morning.

As I was taking in the magical view of the surrounding scenery, I wrote the following: "It is June 22nd I think. I have lost track of time. We've been in Bali for a week now, and have two and a half weeks to go. We've rented a beautiful large, private home in Ubud, with marvelous views of jungle, flowering trees, coconut palm, and rice paddy fields on the horizon. We are nestled in a small gorge surrounded by a multi-layered landscape of green. We have a host family nearby who take care of our every need, and a driver to transport us to other parts of the island. We can even get massages here, if you like it hard like Steve does. We have everything a tropic vacation can offer."

I continued to write, reflecting on my spiritual path: "Emotionally and spirituality, I guess I would refer to the title of the book I am currently reading, *From Seekers to Finders* by Satyam Nadeen.[30] In many ways I feel I am off the seeker train. The best advice I can give myself is to just be present with what is, and let life unfold as it will. More and more, I feel less spiritual even though

Consciousness is all there is. I feel quite ordinary, as though the whole spiritual chase was for naught (it was certainly beautiful though). Again, it seems like all has come full circle, like the Enso. Out of ordinary existence, there was seeking, and more seeking, then just being, then finding, and being, and now ordinary existence. The search is to exhaust itself, and can only cease by itself. It will cease by knowing the deepest level of Truth, not by someone else—not by Joel, David, Tom Kurzka, or even Ramana."

"True recognition can only come from within. Validation can only come from the inner teacher. I have waited for someone else to tell me the truth of my being, even though the experiential insights have so clearly shown who I am, time and time again. I have searched in vain to find freedom. This has kept me in bondage. But when I relax into the Self that I am, my own heart, the search is over. I am the only one that can put this seeking to rest."

The Awakening

Recalling the precise details of my awakening is difficult, partly because my plentiful spiritual experiences earlier had led me to not grasp at the details. Basically, I learned that it was not the experiences in themselves or the particular mind states that were the gems, it was the insights that lingered that were the most meaningful.

About half way into our vacation and after finishing my reading, I experienced a few days of intense boredom. Steve even teased me about being bored in paradise. I slowly surrendered to the deep relaxation, and not having anything scheduled to busy the mind with. We took part in tourist activities, visited temples, and even dressed in traditional attire during some of the holy days, but there was plenty of time to simply relax.

I meditated outside with Steve every morning before the sun rose. We sat under the teak veranda in the dark, as the layers of sound from the jungle would transform the day. The insects would lead the choir, before being joined by a crescendo of birds. Bats would fly around us until the light encouraged their retreat. Slowly the jungle would appear before our eyes, at first only the dark silhouette of palm leaves, then the emerging emerald glow of the gorge below.

My dream life was very active, although I recorded few dreams. And, though I brought my journal, besides the beginning entries, I never recorded anything after that. In fact, there are no journal entries until February of 2009, a year and a half later. This was highly unusual for me, since throughout the years I have logged the details of my spiritual practices and progress. What I recall of the days before the awakening is that there were several vivid dreams, and plenty of naps.

One night, I awoke in the early morning hours and opened my eyes, but did not know where I was. I then realized I was still dreaming, but remained lucid. I watched as the perception of my world started to form together out of dream. Soon, my identity and all the thoughts that make up my life appeared. In a moment of recognition I saw these arising thoughts, arising as Consciousness. While I had seen this before in choiceless awareness meditations, I had never seen it so clearly related to who I was. I was able to see the identity of me, the story, as it was forming. It was as though the waking story of who I am had formed out of dream images. But, it was not a dream I was waking from. It was the "Story of I," the waking dream appearing as my life. I was alertly witnessing this story form, thus I knew I could not be the story that was arising.

I recall thinking this would be a noteworthy entry for my journal, but there was absolutely no movement or desire to record what happened. The insight is what carried forth, while the exact dream images have now faded from my memory. As I got up and started going through the day, it was revealed again and again the truth of who I was, including the transparency of all my important and random thoughts. They were not my doing. Who I was, was being revealed as Consciousness, in the simplicity of the present moment, moment by moment. Yet, nothing was happening, and nothing changed. The Presence, or that unchanging space within, remained the same.

There was nothing profound or spectacular about this revelation. Actually, it was quite ordinary. However, it was also life changing. While daily meditation had been my highest priority for the past five years, this was the first change I noticed. I no longer felt the need or desire to meditate. Instead of getting up early with Steve, as we had been doing, I rolled over and went back to sleep. There simply wasn't the need to meditate any longer, as the clarity and presence is what was there, and my thoughts were no longer a problem.

Now, my interest in meditation has slowly changed over time since our trip. I recognize the value in meditating after taking close to a two-year break from it. Keeping a meditation practice is helpful to stay connected to a spiritual community, and being available to share meditation techniques with others. So, gradually, I have returned to meditating, but never to the degree as when I was a seeker.

There were more changes over time that I noticed, including the major one: I wasn't seeking approval, or validation from my teachers. What I discovered that morning in Bali is one of those mysteries, but the search was over. A relaxed quality took over my inner life, and I knew there was nothing needed to make me more complete and whole. I was That and always have been. I had awakened out of the "Story of I" just long enough to see it arising by itself, and now was free to fully just be in the midst of the dance of life.

Awakening is not something that has ownership, and is nothing we can bring about ourselves, no matter how hard we try. I think it came about because I finally had exhausted the search, and reached a level of surrender, along with a feeling of completion. And there was a part of me that just didn't care any more. Maybe the mind had slowed its chatter through my meditation practice, or the boredom I was feeling had slowed my mind enough to see what was arising. I will never know. Whatever the variables, I got out of my own way just long enough. Then, when the "real world" came flooding back in, as it always does, it was recognized as arising in and being Consciousness.

Before my awakening I certainly had a great depth of understanding, yet there still was the spiritual story—The Seeker. The one trying to understand, striving for a more expansive spiritual experience, seeking validation, and battling her thoughts. This time, my thoughts stopped long enough to have clarity, and when they began again, they were simply recognized that they were not me. I was not the separate identity needing to fight them, judge them, or make a life story based on them. Awakening to the Truth simply happened, no bells or whistles, although certainly I have had plenty of those. At last I knew. The Mountain is within me. I am the inner teacher. I am what I have been seeking.

EPILOGUE

I n the end it is revealed that all the seeking, the invitations to journey deep into the depth of our souls, the struggles, and experiences have all been the movement of Consciousness. We as the seeker are never apart from this nor have we been a separate one, even an individual ego creating it.

So I close this book, not knowing where life will lead me next. Whether I, as this body travels to India, writes more books, talks to others about the spiritual journey, or fully falls into the role of the householder working and awaiting the next paycheck; it does not matter. Whether thoughts creep up with some unanswered questions, debating some past experience or insight, again it does not matter. If a so-called enemy appears, or even if things are going the way I had hoped they would, it does not matter. Whether the sound is too loud, or one I can barely hear; all is arising just as it is meant to be. I am here to experience and witness as before. The journey is to discover who that witness really is. The Zen koan, "if a tree falls in the forest does anyone hear it?" comes to mind. Well, who is there to hear and experience, who is there to witness? Who is here to listen to the Mountain whisper its private messages?

It has become unmistakably clear that the witness, the message, the Mountain, and the tree are all the same. In the end, as my favorite teacher Joel would often say, "You need to go out and find out for yourself." This is so true. No matter how many times I was told where to look, and even what I was looking for, the inward journey is where I found Truth.

No one, and certainly not this book, can satisfy the search. What I have shared, I hope will be helpful in seeing one of the most beautiful insights that finally changed the way I view the spiritual path. God loves the journey, the divine dance of potential union, the yearning heartache of love, and dance of contraction and expansion. This is why the path does not need to be rushed, and even when you feel that you have reached the end, God does not want it to end. There will be some type of deepening, or a return to meditation, a time of sharing the spiritual path with others, so it may be experienced once more.

There is a sweetness to the dance of discovery, whether one takes a path of devotion or the search for Truth. All paths converge as we glimpse what we have been searching for all along. What we end up discovering is that Consciousness never goes anywhere, it is not something that is distant from us, or hidden once our heightened spiritual experiences end: It is here always. It is closer than our own face, closer than our own breath. We are an empty vessel just waiting to realize we are already filled with Consciousness—the complete and lasting Love we have always longed for.

In the continual return to the space within that never changes, we can all discover the Heart of Presence. And, when we approach the end of our searching, it is time to trust our inner teacher, as no outside authority can put an end to seeking. When duality is seen through, there is truly only One. Consciousness is revealed to include all, the manifestation of student, teacher, and even our beloved object of devotion. This is bringing home the Mountain, since the Mountain, or God, is always and forever what we have been seeking outside ourselves. In the end, we simply come home to our own hearts and rest in That.

NOTES

1 Eckhart Tolle is an awakened teacher and author of *The Power of Now*, *Stillness Speaks*, and *A New Earth* who clearly communicates the importance of being present in everyday life. See Resources.

2 See Resources for website and teachings of the Center for Sacred Sciences.

3 See Bibliography. Joel Morwood is the author of *The Way of Selflessness* and *Naked through the Gate*.

4 The *Advaita Vedanta* (or non-dual) teachings is an ancient Hindu philosophy. *Advaita* means non-dual, only one, and refers to Consciousness, Self, or God. *Vedanta* means the realization of Truth, Self-realization, or Consciousness. In *Advaita Vedanta* the seeker focuses on self-inquiry to discover the truth of who they are, and to discover there is only one in Consciousness, meaning that the soul and Brahman (God) are the same.

5 See Resources and Bibliography for website for the teachings of Sri Ramana Maharshi.

6 The Gospel of Thomas quoted *in Dark Night of the Soul: A Masterpiece in the Literature of Mysticism by St. John of The Cross*. Translated by E. Allison Peers, Image Books: Double Day, 1990.

7 Cloud Mountain is a beautiful retreat center located in Castle Rock, Washington, and offers a variety of meditation and spiritual retreats year round. See www.cloudmountain.org.

8 Tom Kurzka is an awakened teacher in the *Advaita Vedanta* tradition. See Resources.

9 *The Tibetan Yogas of Dream and Sleep.* Geshe Tenzin Wangyal Rinpoche. Snow Lion Publications, 1998.

10 The sacred mountain Arunachala, believed to be an embodiment of Shiva, is considered a potent spiritual destination for Hindus and spiritual tourists around the world. Arunachala is located in Tiruvannamalai, India. Ramana Maharshi spent over fifty years living on or near the Mountain following his own awakening as a teenager, until his death in 1950. He sometimes referred to the Mountain as his father, and was considered to be his one attachment. Refer to Resources for the Sri Ramana Maharshi website.

11 See Resources and Bibliography for website and teachings of David Waldman. David Waldman is also the author of *The Wisdom of Love*.

12 *The Spiritual Teachings of Ramana Maharshi.* Sri Ramanasramam, Shambhala Publications, Inc. Boston, Massachusetts, 2004. Also listed in Bibliography.

13 Five Hymns to Sri Arunachala, Sixth Edition. Sri Ramanasramam, Tiruvannamalai, 1982. Also listed in Bibliography.

14 Adyashanti is an awakened Western Teacher with a Zen Buddhist background who shares through public *satsangs*, retreats, and writing the path of *Advaita Vedanta*, non-dual teachings. See Resources for his website website.

15 *The Teachings of Bhagavan Sri Ramana Maharshi in His Own Words.* Arthur Osborne, Sri Ramanasramam, Tiruvannamalai, 2002.

16 The story goes that before Papaji's awakening, he would sometimes try to get away from Ramana, as Ramana's teachings were sometimes annoying to him. However, Ramana would then sit on the cliff above Papaji's Cave, so there was no escaping.

17 The word *darshan* has its original roots in Sanskrit and means to see or to be received into the presence of a holy person.

18 The Four Noble Truths are listed in *How to Solve Our Human Problems: The Four Noble Truths.* Geshe Kelsang Gyatso, Tharpa Publications. U.S. Edition, 2007.

19 *Heart is Thy Name, Oh Lord: Moments of Silence with Sri. Ramana Maharshi.* V.S. Ramana: Sri. Ramanasraman, 2004. Also listed in Bibliography.

20 Papaji (also known as H.W.L. Poonja) was an enlightened teacher of the *Advaita Vedanta* tradition, and was the teacher of Gangaji and many others. Papaji considered Ramana Maharshi to be his most influential teacher.

21 *Matri Vani. From the Wisdom of Sri Anandamayi Ma, Vol. 2.* Shree Shree Anadamayee Charitable Society. Bhadaini, Varanasi. 1977.

22 *No mind, I am the Self: The Lives and Teachings of Lakshmana Swamy and Mathru Sri Sarada.* David Godman. Bhanumathy Ramanadham, Sri Lakshmana Ashram. 1985.

23 See Note 22, Bibliography, and Resources for website information and books by David Godman.

24 There are several references in Hindu and Buddhist teachings of the ego becoming like a burned rope after awakening. The symbolic burned rope still has form, such as a personality, however after awakening it becomes harmless to tie anything up.

25 See note 29, and References for Ramana Maharshi's teachings and website information.

26 *The Spiritual Heart, Bhagavan Ramana Answers.* A.R. Natarajan. Ramana Maharshi Center for Learning. Bangalore, 2005. Also listed in Bibliography.

27 Marlies Cocheret is an awakened teacher, and student of Adyashanti. Her website is www.marliescocheret.com.

28 Dr. Franklin Merrell-Wolff was an awakened teacher in the *Advaita Vedanta* tradition, as well as a brilliant philosopher, and mathematician. See Resources.

29 John Sherman is an awakened teacher in the *Advaita Vedanta* tradition. Visit www.johnsherman.org.

30 Satyam Nadeen is an awakened teacher in the *Advaita Vedanta* tradition and the author of *From Seekers to Finders.* See

www.satyamnadeen.com for information regarding *satsangs* and teachings. See Bibliography.

BIBLIOGRAPHY

A New Earth: Awakening to Your Life's Purpose, Eckhart Tolle. Plume: Penguin Books, 2005.

A Still Forest Pool: The Insight Meditations of Achaan Chah, David Kornfield & Paul Brieter, The Theosophical Publishing House: Quest Printing, 1994.

Awakening the Mind, Lightening the Heart, His Holiness The Dalai Lama. The Library of Tibet. Harper: San Francisco, 1995.

Dark Night of the Soul: A Masterpiece in the Literature of Mysticism by St. John of The Cross, translated by E. Allison Peers, Image Books: Double Day, 1990.

Five Hymns to Sri Arunachala, Sixth Edition, Sri Ramanasramam, Tiruvannamalai, 1982.

From Seekers to Finders: The myth and reality about enlightenment, Satyam Nadeen. Hay House, Inc. Carlsbad, California. 2000.

Heart is Thy Name, Oh Lord: Moments of Silence with Sri. Ramana Maharshi, V.S. Ramana: Sri. Ramanasraman, 2004.

How to Solve Our Human Problems: The Four Noble Truths, Geshe Kelsang Gyatso, Tharpa Publications. U.S. Edition, 2007.

I Am That: Talks with Sri Nisargadatta. Nisargadatta Maharaj, Sudhaker S. Dikshit, and Maurice Frydman.

Introduction to Tantra. The Transformation of Desire, Lama Thubten Yeshe. Wisdom Publications. Boston. 1987.

Matri Vani. From the Wisdom of Sri Anandamayi Ma, Volume 2, Shree Shree Anadamayee Charitable Society. Bhadaini, Varanasi. 1977.

No Boundary: *Eastern and Western Approaches to Personal Growth*, Ken Wilber. Shambhala Publications, Inc. Boston, Massachusetts. 1979.

No mind, I am the Self: The Lives and Teachings of Lakshmana Swamy and Mathru Sri Sarada, David Godman. Bhanumathy Ramanadham,☐Sri Lakshmana Ashram. 1985.

Passionate Presence: *Experiencing the Seven Qualities of Awakened Awareness,* Catherine Ingram. Gotham Books. 2003.

Spectrum of Ecstasy: Embracing the five wisdom emotions of Vajrayana Buddhism, Ngakpa Chogyam and Khandro Dechen. Shambhala, Boston. 2003.

Stillness Speak, Eckhart Tolle. New World Library. Novato, California. 2003.

Surprised by Grace: *A journey beyond personal enlightenment,* Amber Terrell. Audio Edition. True Light Publishing. 2003.

Tao Te Ching, Lao Tsu. Translated by Gia-Fu Feng and Jane English. Vintage Books Edition: Random House, 1997.

The Bhagavad Gita, Translated by Juan Mascaro. Penguin Books. 1962.

The Deeper Wound: Recovering the Soul from Fear and Suffering, Deepak Chopra. Harmony Books: Random House: New York. 2001.

The Diamond in Your Pocket: *Discovering your true radiance,* Gangaji. Sounds True, Inc. Boulder, Colorado. 2005.

The Door to Satisfaction: The Heart Advice of a Tibetan Buddhist Master, Lama Thubten Zopa Rinpoche. Wisdom Publications: Boston, 1994.

The Power of Now. A guide to spiritual enlightenment, Eckhart Tolle. New World Publishing, Novato, California. 1999.

The Spiritual Heart. Bhagavan Ramana Answers, A.R. Natarajan. Ramana Maharshi Center for Learning. Bangalore, 2005.

The Spiritual Teachings of Ramana Maharshi, Sri Ramanasramam. Shambhala Publications, Inc. Boston, Massachusetts, 2004.

The Tibetan Book of Living and Dying: The Revised Edition, Sogyal Rinpoche, Harper Collins Publisher. 1992.

The Tibetan Yogas of Dream and Sleep, Geshe Tenzin Wangyal Rinpoche. Snow Lion Publications. 1998.

The Way of Selflessness: *A practical guide to enlightenment based on the teachings of the World's Great Mystics,* Joel Morwood. Center for Sacred Sciences. Eugene, Oregon. 2009.

The Wisdom of Love: *Talks with David Waldman*, David Waldman. iUniverse, Inc. Lincoln, NE. 2005.

Who am I? The teachings of Bhagavan Sri Ramana Maharshi. Published by T.N. Venkataraman, Sri Ramanasramam, Tiruvannamalai. 1994.

You can be happy no matter what: Five principles for keeping life in perspective, New edition, Richard Carlson. New World Library. Novato, California. 1997.

Zen Mind, Beginners Mind: Informal talks on Zen meditation and practice, Shunryu Suzuki. Weatherhill: New York & Tokyo, 2000.

Zen Essence: The Science of Freedom. Translated and edited by Thomas Cleary. Shambhala Publications: Boston & Shaftesbury, 1989.

RESOURCES

Adyashanti. For teachings, *satsangs*, and contact information visit his website at www.adyashanti.org.

Cathy Rosewell Jonas, author of *Bringing Home the Mountain: Finding the Teacher Within.* For other writing, spiritual blog, meditation techniques, events, and contact information please visit: www.awakeningthespiritualheart.com or www.freeheartpress.com.

David Waldman. Information about teachings, *satsangs*, and contact information is available on his website: www.davidwaldman.org.

Dr. Franklin Merrell Wolff. For information on teachings, books, and events visit www.integralscience.org "Home of the transcendental philosophy of Franklin Merrell-Wolff."

Sri Bhagavan Ramana Maharshi. For information, teachings, and books, please visit the ashram website at www.sriramanamaharshi.org, and the David Godman's website at www.davidgodman.org.

The Center for Sacred Sciences. Explores spirituality from a mystical and scientific perspective. Teachings, including an extensive library of books and resources are offered: www.centerforsacredsciences.org.

Tom Kurzka. For information on *satsangs* offered, visit his website at www.fallintonow.org.